awn Chris Josie Ken Slim Wilma Karen Ed Sophia
ul Dave Mickey Terry Katie Keith Ann Linda Jennifer
ncy Peter John Lillian Emily David Betsy Bob Rick
ard Joan Bernard Charlie Mandel Duke Tim Andrea
onnie Joie Janet Tom Dominique Gavin Mario Pat
ci Claire Jeannette Carol Paul Silvano Michael Joel
my Colin Eda Thomas Tara Pepe Annette Hal Oscar
dy Peter Dominic Brooke Etta Connie Hank Diane
Susan Russell Jean Agnes Jeff Roberto Loise Larry
Mitch Doris Neal Richard Stephen Art Marion Herb
mes Julian Maggie Cathy Millie Steve Paul Denise
Dorothy Tina Anita Gail Suzanne Lou Eric Matt Fritz
Chuck Ari Martha Kyle Theo Pamela Ron Joseph
neth Lionel Larry Ralph Philip Grace Sylvia Judith
rine Pat Mary Aileen Polly G.G. Nicole Lee Susie
ce Sol Penny Spencer Stuart Nicole Rosie Andrew
elli Lisa Lauren Todd Fran Janie Paige Barbara Russ
Thomas Theresa Richard Arlyn Bernadette Charles
Brooke Louis Josephine Robert Avery Jerylin Flim

FRIENDS*

FRIENDS*

*BEARING GIFTS

Foreword by Nancy Kissinger

Interiors Photography by Antoine Bootz

JOSEPH CICIO

POINTED LEAF PRESS

To Christopher Joseph Cicio

Through all his gloriousness of being Christopher, he taught me I could love, and by doing so, what true love feels like.
He taught me that being blessed with the title of father was no small responsibility. He taught me that the love that comes through that responsibility brings pain as well as joy—both experiences I will cherish to my dying day, for they instilled in me an understanding and appreciation that surely could never have come to me without my Christopher.

To Bertrum Heckel

As my first and most gifted clairvoyant, Bertrum told me over 30 years ago that I would be writing a book. He also told me that his timing for predictions could be way off. I told him then he could not be more wrong with the book prediction since I even had difficulty with Thank-You notes.
As always he was right, and I was wrong.

Contents

I have known Joe Cicio for over a quarter of a century. We first met at a dinner, one of the many that my husband and I have enjoyed in Joe's company. Some of these have been in New York, but most have been here in rural Connecticut, where we have a country house very close to Joe's own residence. One of our greatest pleasures is to invite a group of friends to eat with us at Thanksgiving, gathering them around our dining table, and reveling in the lively conversation and laughter that invariably follows. It would be unthinkable not to have Joe with us on such occasions.

No one understands and articulates the value of friendship more sincerely than Joe. Blessed with impeccable taste and style, he has steered his way through a highly successful career as one of the leading creative forces in merchandising whilst always retaining his kindness, sensitivity, and integrity. This is no mean feat in this day and age, and it marks him out as someone with a deep-seated sense of honor and commitment to people. Many of those he met through his professional life have gone on to become close personal friends, with those relationships reflected in the art and objects he has brought together in his beautiful home.

As the years pass, we all increasingly appreciate the value of friendship and the significance of times shared. Whether it is advising me on how to overcome a tricky design issue in the house, or graciously accepting yet another consignment of peonies from my overflowing garden, Joe exemplifies why this is so important. What he has achieved, and presented so elegantly in this book, is something that we should all aspire to: Invest in our friendships, collecting experiences and beautiful things as we go along, and then celebrate the richness of the memories that these bring.

OPPOSITE Fashion designer Bill Blass was—after her husband, Secretary of State and diplomat Henry Kissinger—the escort of choice for the philanthropist Nancy Kissinger, when she attended black-tie events in New York City.

When I Have Fears

When I have fears, as Keats had fears,
Of the moment I'll cease to be
I console myself with vanished years
Remember laughter, remembered tears,
And the peace of the changing sea.
When I feel sad, as Keats felt sad,
That my life is so nearly done
It gives me comfort to dwell upon
Remembered friends who are dead and gone
And the jokes we had and the fun.
How happy they are I cannot know
But happy am I who loved them so.
—Noel Coward, from *Collected Verse*

I was in my early twenties when I came across this poem written by Noel Coward just days before his unexpected death in March of 1973. From the first reading, it embodied for me a passionate appreciation for friends and relationships that we are blessed to be part of as we journey through this amazing adventure called life. This book is intended to be a celebration of some of my many relationships and all the valued experiences I have been privileged to cherish to this day. This book will share with you an important lesson about just how we might be able to hold in our hearts the memories of these relationships and experiences: How a lifetime of collecting objects can serve as the vehicle for this remembering, hopefully without sadness but rather with joy. The objects in this book are not featured for their monetary value. Their value is purely in the relationships associated with each of them and the stories of how they came to be part of my life's journey.

A single glance at a particular object can bring those we have loved back to us, even after the day-to-day contact with the people themselves is long past. The events and adventures described in these profiles began, without me necessarily realizing, at the time, that such a rewarding and valuable experience was taking place. Whether by divine intervention or sheer serendipity, my professional and personal lives proved to include the company of some of the finest fellow travelers I could ever have hoped to have.

Being born in Brooklyn, New York, was the first gift to my life, although I don't think I was able to see it as such back then. I think it was because Brooklynites were what I would describe as "real people"—hard working, with no pretense, and very family-oriented. It seemed like everyone had some sort of job that helped get food on the family table. An attack on one was an attack on all, and respect for others was a normal part of daily life. Every passerby

OPPOSITE On a business trip to Florence in the fall of 1996, I enjoyed people-watching, one of my favorite pastimes.

would extend a greeting and offer a smile. It was these "real people" who collectively helped shape who I was and who I later became. To this day, I feel proud to say, "I was born in Brooklyn."

Growing up in a totally dysfunctional Italian family helped set the stage of appreciation for what was to follow years later. Even now, whenever I watch reruns of *The Godfather* or *The Sopranos*, my early memories of childhood come flooding back to me. I found both dramatizations amazingly accurate in every detail. There I was, one of those kids running around with my cousins at *The Godfather*'s opening wedding scene. When Tony Soprano had Sunday dinner, I could almost smell the tomato gravy. No good Sicilian would ever say tomato sauce—it was always called gravy in our family, just as pasta was always referred to as macaroni, regardless of its shape. Everything seemed to revolve around food, with the conversation at most meals being the menu for the next meal, which was invariably just a few hours later. None of the cooks in our family ever followed printed recipes and I don't remember ever seeing a cookbook until I had my own home and started to worship Julia Child. For my mother and aunts, the knowledge of how to cook and what ingredients to use was passed down orally and learned by watching older family members as they created masterpieces in their kitchens.

This was, however, a very dangerous area in which to tread. My mother was one of seven children, five sisters and two brothers. The culinary competition was tough, and woe to anyone who complimented one of my aunts on her gravy. "And what's wrong with MY gravy?" would be the instant response from my outraged, red-faced mother. As a child, I used to love hanging out in the kitchen on Sunday while my mother prepared the large pot of tomato gravy. Meatballs and sausages were always involved, but generally my older sister Theresa and I were told to keep away from the cooking and so stealing juicy morsels was not easy. However, Theresa and I knew all too well that part of my mother's Sunday routine was to have a shower after her early morning meal preparation. We would wait until we heard the water running in the shower and then run into the kitchen and try to steal meatballs out of the simmering pot on the stove. Our inexperience at covering our tracks—and all that messy tomato gravy—meant that my mother knew exactly what was going on while she was out of the kitchen. There would be much yelling when she went back into the kitchen, but I must say I think she very much enjoyed it, because to her it meant that we loved her food so much we could not wait any longer. For my sister and myself, the effort was worth the trauma.

George Bernard Shaw wrote that youth is wasted on the young. There is no doubt that young people take life's blessings for granted, and I must have been well into my 30s before I realized that I had been blessed in so many ways. There were hardships too, of course, but I honestly have never viewed them as such. In the early years, I had little outside experience with which to compare anything, giving me a wonderful excuse to proceed on my journey with a light heart and a positive spirit. A sense of family and the joy of relationships were with me from the start. My father definitely had his own agenda; he was seldom with us as a family and unfortunately had no parental instinct in any sense of the word—amazing, since he fathered eight children. I finally grew to understand that fathering children did not make one a parent. Parenting did. His first love, it seemed, was always business, and the desired financial rewards that hopefully would follow. Yet my hard-working mother, two sisters, many Italian

ABOVE My sister Theresa and I were captured in our new Easter outfits at the Brooklyn Botanical Gardens, in 1950.

aunts, uncles, and countless cousins all instilled in me the joy of family in so many forms, something that has proved to be a recurring theme throughout my life. My experience with my family instilled in me my love of relationships and their power to usher us through even the most difficult times. I also grew to appreciate that a good sense of humor could very well be the most important ingredient in any recipe of survival and growth.

Much to the surprise of all those who thought they knew me, I found myself at the doors of a monastic Benedictine priory right after graduating from high school. I had grown up and been educated in Catholic schools for most of my young life and it was that deep joy of belonging and divine intervention that I believe brought me to God's house. Saint Benedict founded his eponymous order in about 528 in Monte Cassino, Italy, and the great attraction for me was that Saint Benedict had expressly wanted each of his order's monasteries to be considered like a family home. The monks were the family, with the abbot or prior as the father. In his writings, Saint Benedict stated that communal life in a monastery should be viewed as a complete egg yolk, with each of the elements combining to make the whole. I knew none of this at such an early age, but knocked on the priory door regardless. Whether I was there by good fortune or divine intervention is still open to speculation. After almost three years as a monk—an experience I cherish to this day—I returned to the secular world. I had little idea of how to proceed with my life, but faith and a former high school counselor somehow combined to guide me to the doors of Lord & Taylor, the New York specialty store. "You're very creative

ABOVE Lord & Taylor, on Manhattan's Fifth Avenue, is one of the most famous specialty stores in the world. When I was in my early twenties, I remember seeing Lady Bird Johnson, the First Lady, walking in to do her Christmas shopping.

and should try to get a job in window display," my former high school counselor advised. I had no idea what Mrs. Martha Schain was actually trying to suggest, let alone what window display was. The counselor sensed this uncertainty on my part and suggested that I take a display course at a school in New York that had a working relationship with Lord & Taylor. I was about 20 years old and petrified that I now had to earn a living and try to build a life for myself. With no encouragement or financial help from my immediate family, and after almost three years of total security at the priory, I was very much overwhelmed in terms of the future, but I heeded the counselor's helpful advice. I enrolled in the art school and loved every minute of it. It seems I did very well and as a result, at graduation, was one of two students out of a class of 50 that was offered a part-time position at Lord & Taylor in their window display department. I could never have guessed that that first day at Lord & Taylor in 1964 was to play such a defining role in my life.

It was an unbelievably exciting time in retailing. From the 1940s through most of the 1980s, the retail-merchandising buyers were considered gods, almost more powerful and influential in the retail arena than the actual CEOs of the store itself. The buyers carried enormous responsibility for the bottom line of any respected retail establishment and also possessed the power to make or break any emerging merchandising manufacturer in their marketplace. Their offices, through which they walked dozens of times a day, were often carved out of the stockroom spaces directly behind the selling floor. This ensured they had

ABOVE When I was 20 years old, I was completely in awe that I was actually working inside Lord & Taylor's famous Christmas windows. It was a thrill I still recall today. "Totally show biz," was what I remember thinking at the time.

first-hand contact with the product, the consumer, and the staff, which also meant they had to know their business inside out. This is difficult if not impossible to accomplish today in an office tower while in front of a computer, often miles away from the selling floor. In a sense, I think it's fair to say that the elite merchants like Stanley Marcus, Dorothy Shaver, Geraldine Stutz, Adam Gimbel and the like were the retail "computers" of their time. The selling floor was everything and the buyers were true merchants in every sense of the word. They made us, as consumers, want to buy the products they were offering. They made shopping more than just a process to fill a need. They made it a social activity, and presented their wares so creatively that they generated an environment of entertainment.

I actually think I got the job at Lord & Taylor because I was the tallest student and stood out from all the other candidates. I was hired as a part-time extra in the window display department, two days a week, with my main responsibility being to keep the floors clean and shuttle between the 38th Street deli and the store's display department with coffee and iced tea for the executives. It would be difficult to appreciate how truly naive I was at the time, only months after my monastic studies. When a co-worker would refer to one of the other department staff as being gay, I wondered what the big deal was, assuming that "gay" meant that he was just very happy. My favorite task was being dispatched down the street to the best ribbon store in the world, Hyman Hendler. There was not a fashion designer in the world of any worth who did not walk through their door. And it was just steps from the Lord & Taylor side door. It was here that four-foot ten-inches tall Sadie presided over the selling floor. She was a

ABOVE Cici Kempner, standing to my left, was my guest at my very first black-tie Macy's flower show event in 1977.

real force to be reckoned with, but thankfully she liked me because I reminded her of her grandson, so she would often cut extra ribbon and tell me to take it to my girlfriend as a gift. I still have many of those ribbons, which had been imported from all over the world. Some of them can no longer be purchased anywhere.

Because I found it so very exciting and was learning so much, I managed to hold onto my part-time post for well over a year, until a full-time position became available. It was just too special to be there, and somehow I knew I was part of something that could not be duplicated. Much to my delight, I was finally appointed as a mannequin boy, earning $60 a week. You can be sure I was the best mannequin boy ever. I loved every single minute of it and could not wait for Sunday to be over so I could return for the start of the working week on Monday. The highlight of each Monday was always at the department store's fashion counter, where talented executives of a rather flamboyant persuasion would recount episodes from many of the top comedy shows on television and Broadway, to hilarious perfection. Those extraordinarily creative individuals would rival any sitcom actor of today with their flair and humor, and I have no doubt that the stars they impersonated—such as Lucille Ball and Carol Burnett—would have been both impressed and flattered. Thursday evening was the best. That was window installation day and we worked late into the night and often into the early hours of Friday morning. At suppertime, which was always held in the window department, some of the staff would dress in drag (I'd never even heard of drag until then) and would put on a show for the rest of us. My all-time favorite was when Bobby dressed up as Jeanette MacDonald—blonde curls, parasol and all, and Tom—a good deal taller—was in a Canadian Mountie uniform, singing "When I'm Calling You." If only the iPhone had existed then.

There are just no words to describe the sense of fun, laughter, and camaraderie these performances generated. That's when I decided that retailing and display was real show business, of a different kind perhaps from Broadway, but show business nonetheless. It had a very serious side to it, of course, but it never felt like work to me. I realized very quickly that I wanted to be part of it for the long term and hopefully make my mark in life professionally through retail. For a young, uncluttered mind, it was a profoundly exciting and stimulating environment in which to learn and develop, not least because of the talented and inspirational people I found myself working alongside. Each and every day further awakened the creative and merchandising talents that I truly had had no idea were within me until then. At the same time, it quickly became evident that my new career surroundings helped instill a sense of confidence in me that would never have been realized in Brooklyn.

The Lord & Taylor window display department was located in the sub-basement, directly across the aisle from the handbag department stockroom. There sat Cecile "Cici" Blum Kempner, one of the most powerful buyers in the industry. She operated from an old black-painted wooden desk in the middle of the stockroom, with her assistant's desk facing hers. Cici also had a fancy office on an upper executive floor, but the only time she ever sat there was to have her hair cut in privacy, about once a month. The stockroom was her world, and she was compelled by her own passions to be right at the epicenter of all goings-on. Cici did not work because she needed to. She came from a privileged background in Galveston, Texas, and had a lovely apartment on Park Avenue, where I was often a guest at her many small dinner parties, and also invited to use her guest room for late nights when she was traveling abroad. Since she traveled a great deal, and I lived in Queens at the time, this was a dream come true.

To my young, impressionable mind, Cici's apartment was right out of the movies. I had never before seen an apartment in which the elevator opened directly into the entrance hall, or an apartment building where you had to pass six doormen in impressive uniforms even to get to the elevator. If that were not enough, Cici had a very well-known retail celebrity cousin who attended many of her small dinner parties with his lovely wife Linda. His name was Stanley Marcus. At first, I had no idea who he was, other than a very chic, soft-spoken older gentleman and a relative of Cici's, but once I realized that he was the son of the founder of the specialty department store, Neiman Marcus, and its current CEO, I would sit at the table in awe, hanging onto his every word as he shared his experiences of running a retail dynasty. I would walk away from each and every dinner with a jewel of a lesson in retailing. Stanley, as I became privileged to call him, taught me a great deal and, as the years rolled on and my career started to advance, to my amazement a handwritten note of congratulations would arrive from Stanley every time I received a promotion at Lord & Taylor and, later, at Macy's. I never did understand how he learned of each promotion, but he did. Whilst spending money was not Cici's favorite pastime, she was always extremely generous to her small family of friends. When I bought my first house, totally on the spur of the moment, Cici was one of the very first friends I was dying to tell. She immediately expressed her concern, as I was making a very small salary at Lord & Taylor at the time and, while I was a very hard worker and had a number of freelance jobs that more than doubled my income, Cici wasted no time in reminding me that freelance is just that: freelance, with no guarantee of a return engagement. Even so, nothing could convince me that buying the house was not the right thing to do. When you're young, everything seems possible, which makes just about nothing impossible.

One Sunday afternoon, I invited Cici to lunch with a few friends in my new home: a $40,000 prefab house on an acre of land in Wilton, Connecticut. I was so inexperienced at the time that I hadn't even realized that it was a Sears prefab. I thought it was the best thing I had ever seen, mainly because it was now mine. Cici came through the front door with a package under her arm, which in itself was unusual. I hadn't been expecting a gift, but "Here, open it," she said, "and if you don't like it, I want it back." Inside the wrapping was a beautiful painting of a shoreline and the sea beyond. Cici had purchased the painting at an art auction in Florence while on a recent buying trip to Europe. It was painted by an English artist in the latter part of the 19th century, and Cici identified with it because it reminded her of her hometown of Galveston, Texas. I did not own a single painting at the time, and to this day I am not sure if I love it because I think it is a truly wonderful painting, or because Cici loved me enough to spend money on me. Either way, it is one of my most cherished possessions, emblemmatic of my relationship with Cici, which is also one of my greatest treasures. I fervently believe that all those years ago she saw something in me that I even now find difficulty seeing in myself.

OPPOSITE I stood for hours across the street from Macy's on 34th Street, looking at the imposing retail giant after being offered a job there, thinking it was a once-in-a-lifetime opportunity. "Go for it! It can only get better," I thought.

Macy's Fashions The Cellar to Pepper Up Sales

THE NEW LOOK: Macy's unveiled its plans for Herald Square, N.Y., housewares dept. The Celler at the Chicago Housewares Exposition. In attendance were, top right, (left to right) Joe Cicio, visual display director, Teresa Mottoros, merchandise manager and Gordon Cooke, senior v-p, sales promotion; (Right) David Kagan, merchandise coordinator for The Cellar; (left), Ed Finkelstein, Macy's president, and (far left) Art Reiner (left) senior v-p, merchandising, Macy's.
Photos by Bruce Paulson

CHICAGO — It isn't called a basement, heaven forbid, it's The Cellar. And Macy's New York, in an unusual move, chose an evening during the summer housewares exposition to show suppliers its plans for the eagerly awaited Herald Square housewares revamp.

The preview, which took place at a cocktail-hour fete in the Gold Coast Room of the barococo Drake Hotel, was hosted by Edward S. Finkelstein, president of the New York-based merchandising empire.

"To survive in New York, you have to be very good," Finkelstein said in opening remarks made to a wall-to-wall crowd of 600. "We don't want to survive, we want to prosper. The Cellar will have a large setting — the appropriate, contemporary setting we've learned will move more goods."

Finkelstein said Macy's believes the "color, style and fashion" in contemporary housewares merchandise affords "the excitement and opportunity we want to exploit. We're going to help the concept of housewares along with a major fashion department."

Renderings of The Cellar on display at the Drake previewed a natural wood and stucco arcade of windowed shops, each one with its own separate entrance but all interconnected inside.

CUTLERY, COOKWARE, baskets and tabletop shops will be part of the many single-theme boutiques. Each will have its own color motif for instant identification. Ceiling banners will earmark shop openings for customers strolling a ceramic-tiled promenade.

A store official said that housewares will occupy 35 per cent more space in The Cellar. The merchandise will be featured along the 34th St. and Broadway sides of the store. Across The Cellar's shop-strewn street, gourmet food stores, a stationery boutique and, eventually, a restaurant will be located.

The Cellar is only part of a whole new facelift planned for the Herald Square store. A renovated domestics department will open in September. The Cellar will show itself in early October with additional departmental renewals dotting the horizon.

TABLETOP WILL MOVE into the fifth floor quarters vacated by housewares. The budget store that occupied the basement until recently is being eliminated. Concurrent with the return of housewares to the bottom of the store — "an updated homecoming," Finkelstein termed it — the retailing giant is striving to shake off the bargain-shop image that, until recently, appeared to provide the focus of much of the

store's merchandising thrust.

The preview party Macy's threw for its suppliers was done with "color, style and fashion."

"We decided in January it might be a nice thing to turn the tables a little bit and have a party to introduce our suppliers to The Cellar," explained a store official. "We get them all in one place so infrequently, we thought this might be nice."

BESIDES MERRY-MAKING manufacturers at the preview, representatives from the nationwide Macy's family were out in full force.

The New York store was represented by Art Reiner, senior vice-president, merchandising; Gordon Cooke, senior vice-president, sales promotion; Teresa Mottoros, merchandise vice-president directly responsible for The Cellar's activities, and Joseph Cicio, visual display director, plus a slew of buyers and special events people.

Senior vice presidents and buyers from Bamberger's, Macy's sister chain, and from all Macy's divisions speckled the crowd of party-goers. Lots of attention went to the San Francisco crowd whose store pioneered The Cellar concept when Finkelstein was president of that division.

It was also thanks to Cici that I began my lifetime of collecting beautiful objects. A couple of years later I was planning my very first trip to Europe. Lord & Taylor had a travel agency on the 10th floor called Ask Mr. Foster, and once I had saved what I hoped was enough money, I asked him. For $460, I got myself a 21-day visit to London, Paris, and Rome, with hotel accommodation and one meal a day included. I could barely contain my excitement and rushed off to share my enthusiasm with my friend Cici. She was just as delighted, but had some profound advice to offer. "Listen to me carefully," she said. "You have a great eye and talent, so I want you to promise me that, with this very first trip and all those that follow, you will purchase one beautiful object on each trip for yourself. It need not be expensive, but with your taste and style I know it will be beautiful. As a result, after many years, and when I will be long gone, you will have a wonderful home full of beautiful things which, for you, will forever be associated with those travels and the memories of cherished relationships experienced along the way. There will be countless times when you will look at an object in your home and recall the magical experience of when and how you acquired it and whom you were with. The love or admiration you have for the individual will be associated with that one thing." But the real gift is that the relationship will last forever. I cannot help thinking how pleased she would be that I have learned my lesson well and am passing it on, as she did through me.

On that first trip, she managed to get me to join her in Florence, which she was visiting on a market trip. While Cici was working during the day, her friends would guide me through many of the amazing museums. I'm not sure I had ever even been inside a museum before, but I certainly understood how lucky I was to have these friendships and contacts. I remember thinking that, someday and somehow, I would try to do for others as Cici had done for me.

The years passed and my career at Lord & Taylor was progressing well, I thought. I was very happy where I worked and had no intention of changing jobs. But what often happens in these situations is that individuals within the industry start bringing up your name in talking to others in the industry. At one point, I had refused several requests to interview at Saks Fifth Avenue. One evening shortly thereafter, at dinner at the Russian Tea Room, I shared with Cici the Saks interview story. She was furious, scolding me severely for not going through with the interview. I quickly understood that she was trying to teach me how to be an adult in the business world. Several months later, Macy's approached me and requested an interview. My initial reaction was that if I had not accepted the interview with Saks I was surely not about to take one with Macy's (which was by then a tired shadow of its former glory). Then I thought of Cici and her advice and became frankly worried that she would disown me if I did not follow through.

I went ahead with the interview basically just to be able to tell Cici that I had done so. That one event proved to be a most important turning point in my career and life. After months of meetings and further interviews, I was finally offered a job at Macy's—which I accepted. I started my new career there on February 2, 1976, and it was a move that would prove to be the most important decision of my young life. Little did I know that I would end up working

OPPOSITE Edward S. Finkelstein's innovative concept for the new Cellar at Macy's rocked the world of retailing.

with some of the most amazingly capable people in the retail community and become part of a professional team that would go on to build greatness in that world. Many of us very quickly became a family and what I learned through exposure to these great talents could never be found in any textbook today. It was not just about merchandising, but the entire business structure of a complex and exciting industry. While at Macy's, I was exposed to inspirational executives in the areas of retail merchandising, finance, operations, human resources, marketing, product development, store planning, and design. But Macy's had a uniquely talented management team, at that time led by the CEO, Edward S. Finkelstein, who possessed an unusual instinct for understanding and appreciating the importance of the creative edge. Ed wanted shopping to be entertaining and understood the concept and power of impulse purchasing through creative presentation and store environment before it was even an industry term. He worked on the basis that, to be competitive, a brand had to be distinctive, that merchandising in itself was not enough, and that the distinctive environment of a store had to be partnered with a dynamic presentation.

Ed's singular insight and vision gave Macy's an edge over the competition, helping develop a profitable department store brand across our nation through a combination of unique talents and an innovative, creative culture. Through it all, I have never forgotten that, if it were not for Cici Kempner, I wouldn't have been part of this remarkable team.

Yet as much as I adored my work, I adored my young son Christopher much more.

ABOVE The display of the Bill Blass bed linens collection was a major success. OPPOSITE A newspaper clipping included the Bill Blass collection, top, that started the positive press that never seemed to stop for many years.

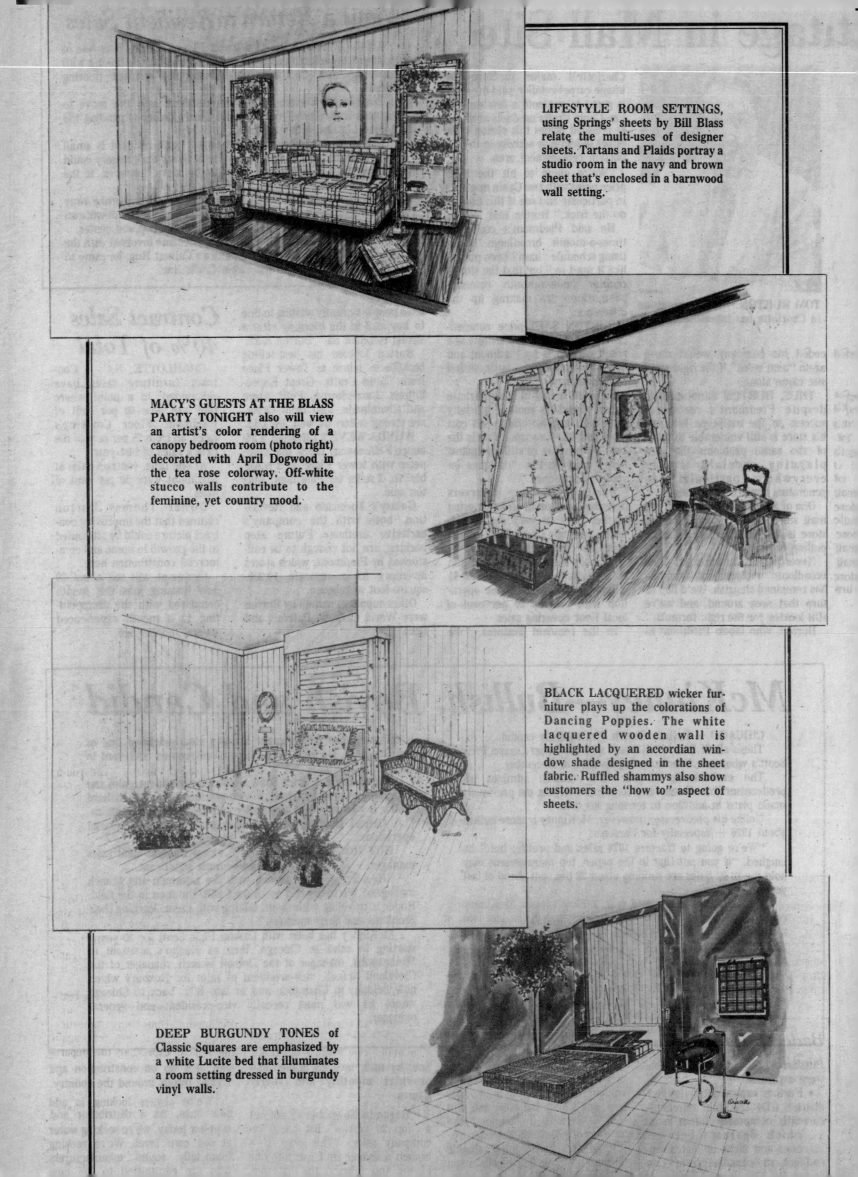

LIFESTYLE ROOM SETTINGS, using Springs' sheets by Bill Blass relate the multi-uses of designer sheets. Tartans and Plaids portray a studio room in the navy and brown sheet that's enclosed in a barnwood wall setting.

MACY'S GUESTS AT THE BLASS PARTY TONIGHT also will view an artist's color rendering of a canopy bedroom room (photo right) decorated with April Dogwood in the tea rose colorway. Off-white stucco walls contribute to the feminine, yet country mood.

BLACK LACQUERED wicker furniture plays up the colorations of Dancing Poppies. The white lacquered wooden wall is highlighted by an accordian window shade designed in the sheet fabric. Ruffled shammys also show customers the "how to" aspect of sheets.

DEEP BURGUNDY TONES of Classic Squares are emphasized by a white Lucite bed that illuminates a room setting dressed in burgundy vinyl walls.

From his birth and adoption in 1990, he was my number one priority, bringing me untold joy and with it a sense of great responsibility to do right by him. At the same time, for various reasons, ranging from a weak national economy to poor management decisions, great career opportunities were placed at my front door. Change happened, and my career took a dramatic upward turn at that point. As a result, I went on to enjoy professional challenges that I couldn't even have fantasized about a few years earlier.

In 1992, I was appointed CEO of I. Magnin, following in the shoes of my good friend Rosemarie Bravo. It was an awesome experience, and after almost three years, Donna Karan convinced me to join her company as president of retail development, store planning, and visual merchandising. I was there for a little over a year when Sun International wooed me into the position of president of retail development for their properties, with Atlantis in the Bahamas being the jewel in the crown. I was able to develop their entire retail presence in their most important property.

Then, it was on to the joy of working with Jane Terker when I became president of Penhaligon's while at the same time overseeing the Erno Laszlo business in Europe. After a few wonderful years, it was clear that I needed to spend more time with Christopher, who was by now becoming a typical teenager. So, after an amazing stint with the best possible exposure to just about every facet of the fashion and retailing markets, I decided to stay in New York and

PREVIOUS PAGES In Paris in 1977, I, far right, was part of a group of "men in suits" that included Edward S. Finkelstein, far left, Art Reiner, Joel Schneider, Frank Duroff, and Bruce Binder. We loved every minute of our working mission. ABOVE Audrey Hepburn adored children and worked tirelessly for UNICEF on their behalf. The morning of her Macy's Corner Shop celebrity room opening, she insisted on being photographed with my son, Christopher.

Connecticut while consulting for others. Little did I know that this would bring me to the door of Highgrove House, the country home of HRH Prince Charles.

Looking back, Cici Kempner was absolutely on target with her great advice on collecting and ensuring a lifetime of memories. I have had many homes through the years—I guess I'm a restless soul. This may be due in part to my Dad, who was a successful real estate investor. In each of my homes, I have always tried to surround myself with beautiful objects that speak to me in terms of their associations with places, events and, most importantly, people. I get so much pleasure from the transformation of each residence. I love walking through, envisioning immediately where the potential might be. There is so much to consider and it seems to happen so fast in my head. My greatest regret is that my father never lived to see how I took my first one-acre prefab ranch to a 360-acre stone castle estate and back again. He would have loved it, and hopefully felt that all he taught me had somehow landed in the right place.

I very much enjoy entertaining at home. Although images of my homes have been published many times in various publications, little gives me greater joy than having a guest or visitor comment on a particular object in a given room—allowing me to share with them the story behind how it got there. I always want my homes to be both inviting and unpretentious. A home should appear to a guest as if they have just walked into a lifetime of valued experiences and relationships. In my view, when we walk through a home we are walking through a life. If I want a stage set, I can go to the movies, a Broadway show, or a four-star-hotel lobby. I

ABOVE My first black tie event at the invitation of HRH Prince Charles was at Highgrove, his country estate, in 2006. Robert Higdon, far left, ensured that no detail was forgotten. I was honored to be seated next to the Duchess of Cornwall.

always look for the patina in a room. That simply tells me that people live here, hopefully with animals. With two dogs in my home, you can be sure we have patina to spare. When Joan Rivers first walked into the house I had completed for her, she called me immediately. "I feel like I have lived here all my life," was the first thing she said. The second was, "Please get over here so we can open some champagne." The call came at about 10 pm on a Friday night and I got back to my own home about 2 am the following morning.

Aside from good health and family, I can think of little that is more meaningful in life than the experience of valued relationships. Through the experience of living, I have been privileged to enjoy the love, friendship, guidance, company, and support of very many outstanding individuals. They did not have to be celebrities, but they did have to be special. The profiles in this book highlight a few of the great joys these people have brought to me, and how I continue to remember each and every one of them through the memories inspired by objects collected through a most eventful lifetime, while recalling that, in the words of Anthony J. D'Angelo: "The most important things in life aren't things." Would this book have happened were it not for all these relationships, or for the gift of being befriended by Cici Blum Kempner, with her love and caring to share her wisdom? Absolutely not. Of that, I'm sure.

ABOVE Chris and I would go away alone every year before he was to start the school year. In 1999, we decided on a week of fishing in Nantucket. Chris caught many fish, and I caught a cold. OPPOSITE When I walked into Theiren, my favorite antiques showroom in San Francisco, and saw this Empire mantelpiece, I had to have it for my Manhattan apartment. Bill Blass and I would often get into trouble in such places. He would often give me the push I needed.

THE
GARDEN

OVERLEAF The original one-story house to the far left was just fine for weekends but not spacious enough for entertaining. The two-story structure add-on to the right gave me exactly what I had envisioned: A proper home and the always-needed project. PAGES 34–35 When I first bought the house there was absolutely no landscaping, no pool, no stonework, and no points of interest to gaze upon. But with the view of the church steeple, I felt that there was tremendous potential. PAGES 36–37 I believe that every country home should have a secret garden. Asta and Piper, my wire hair terriers, are the primary residents of the one I made specially for them. They allow me to take my morning coffee there if I share my toasted bagel with them. PAGES 38–39 From the first day that I visited the property, I envisioned a post-and-beam barn located to the right of the long drive that leads to the main house.

To have known Joan Rivers is to understand that not only was the Academy Award-nominated documentary in 2010, *Joan Rivers—A Piece of Work,* exceptionally well done, but also that its title could not have been more perfectly crafted. Joan Rivers was truly a one-of-a-kind force of nature. I have known many people who have given their all to pursue their passions and advance their careers, but to my mind, few have come close to Joan in either department. She was blessed with great talent and an amazing capacity for endless hard work, as well as for living life to its fullest.

From the late 1970s, I had met Joan at a number of private dinner parties or events in New York, but it was only in about 2001 that I began to know the real Joan. By then she had decided that she wanted a weekend home in the country, but all she ever did was work, which she absolutely loved. She was then in her early 70s and perhaps thinking about doing a bit less and enjoying her friends a bit more.

Joan had started her search—she and I had really gotten to know each other well, and viewed properties with her close friend Tommy Corcoran, often bringing her then-partner Orin Lehman along for the ride. More than a year went by with little success. One day, a mutual friend told Joan that she should buy my own newly renovated house in Connecticut. The obvious problem with this idea at the time was that my house was not on the market, but after many conversations, the mutual friend convinced me to let Joan come to visit one Saturday, "just to take a look." Who could resist the opportunity to have Joan Rivers in their home? To make the visit more civilized and less like a business experience, I suggested that she come for lunch. Joan agreed and arrived with Tommy and Orin. I very much enjoyed her company and was impressed with her as a person. She walked around the house and property, said the customary "oohs" and "aahs," and then went back to the city. I never expected any follow-up after this fun visit.

Several days later, I got a call from her devoted assistant, Jocelyn Pickett, asking me how much I wanted for my house. I tried to explain that it was not for sale and that I—and indeed, the house—had barely gotten over the renovation experience I had just completed. But anyone who knew Joan would appreciate that the word "no" was simply not in her vocabulary. She persisted via Jocelyn, who made endless calls to me. I finally gave in and came up with a number that I thought was astronomical but totally justified, since it was a completely renovated home, both inside and out. Joan later confided in me that she thought my asking price was insane, but what most people don't understand about evaluating the price of a house is that it's not just based on what you see, but also on what you cannot see and do not know. Very often, this involves issues to do with the running and maintenance of a property, and in my case I had used the best local tradesmen, with whom I'd developed superb relationships and who would move mountains for me. I heard nothing back from Joan for many months thereafter and thought little of it. I think I was even a little pleased at the time that I wouldn't be having to move.

Then came the call. There was a message at my New York home telling me that she had found a house near mine and wanted me to do the interiors. I called back, got Jocelyn, and tried to explain that I did not do house interiors as a living. Yet Joan's timing was uncannily

OPPOSITE Comedienne Joan Rivers gave me the branches that add a visual interest to the exterior of the barn.

perfect. I was working in Florida at the time as the CEO of a jewelry company, which we had just sold, and I was due back in the Northeast in a few months' time. Even so, as much as I love interior design, retailing and merchandising would always be my first love and I had no intention of embarking on a new career as an interior designer.

Jocelyn continued to call me, saying how Joan loved my taste, and was very taken with my style of collecting and by how I had managed to pull everything together. She particularly loved that the house looked and felt like it had evolved through years of good times and happy travels. I was hugely flattered, of course, but had no intention of taking on such a project.

Meanwhile, Joan being Joan refused to take no for an answer. She insisted that I at least come and meet her at her new house the next weekend since we would both be in the area. "I just want your point of view," she said. I said yes, intrigued perhaps by her warning that it was "the ugliest house in Connecticut." She said it looked like a Benihana Japanese Steakhouse. I was raised in a real estate culture and so could never resist going to see just about any house. From when I was about eight years old, my father would take me along when he was touring properties. I remember being told that I was to say nothing, but just observe and listen. When we got back in the car, he would tell me everything good and bad about the property we had just seen. He taught me how to look at a house from the foundation to the curb, training my eye in the art of real estate observation. It is just that, an art, and those lessons have proved very helpful in my life and throughout my career.

I knew exactly where Joan's soon-to-be new house was—within walking distance to the house of my dear friend Bill Blass and only a five-minute ride from my own place, so I agreed to meet her there for what proved to be an unforgettable visit. The mile-long driveway up to the house was magical enough, and when you got to the top of the 80-acre property, the existing house commanded the most amazing position, with totally captivating 180-degree views. Joan had arrived just 30 seconds before me and I was thrilled by the sight of her getting out of a black stretch limo in a red fox fur coat and five-inch Manolo Blahnik heels, complete with an Hermès handbag, just like a page out of *Women's Wear Daily*. Not exactly country gear, but wonderful all the same and with great star quality, of course.

We exchanged greetings and, as is usually my style, I proceeded to tell Joan that she was absolutely correct. This was indeed the ugliest house in Connecticut. She laughed and told me that the architect had apparently been a student of Frank Lloyd Wright. "Shame he didn't study more," was my retort. She loved that comment and used it for years after when she did her before-and-after tours of the house for guests. The house was truly awful, even if the property and views were wonderful, and the house actually got worse inside. My biggest problem in these situations is that I am really very good at looking past the ugly and envisioning the lovely. I want to attack, even if the place is not mine. My impulse is always to make it right. I'm the guy who will go in and rearrange a hotel room and sometimes even the lobby. But on this occasion I said very little. Meanwhile, Joan kept at it, saying how I simply had to do this for her. She was a very effective negotiator.

OPPOSITE Joan Rivers had a wonderful smile that could light up a room—because it was real. She loved being with people but, perhaps even more than that, she loved being with her dogs, including Max, one of her rescues.

"Ok," I said, "What do you want here?" She looked at me intently. "I want a Connecticut country home," came the quick reply. "I want warm and cozy." Her eyes sparkled. "And I want to eat with my friends in the kitchen," she continued. I finally asked her to leave me for 15 minutes so I could walk around on my own. It was more to keep her off my back and be able to think than anything else, but as I went from room to room it all began to fall into place. I imagined a French door here, a fireplace there, a wall removed in this room, and perhaps a skylight in that one. Maybe some antique beams there. A vision for Joan's country home started to come together in my mind. I love that very first encounter, where no man has gone before. It could be wonderful, I thought.

I then sat Joan down and said I would consider doing the house for her so long as she agreed to five conditions. The most important was that she entrusted me with giving her a complete presentation of the entire house, and that she agreed to never bother me with changes or buy anything for the house that I had not blessed myself. Another condition was that there would be no contract binding either party. She could decide at any time that it was over and so could I. She quickly agreed to everything with great enthusiasm and gratitude. Afterwards, once I'd gotten to know her better, I discovered that she had never intended to keep that promise about not making any changes. Even so, I was the perfect match for Joan and knew that in many ways I was as strong a personality as she was. I also had the added security of knowing that she needed me more than I needed her. To me, this project was only worth taking on if it was fun and emotionally rewarding and, to both our credit, it proved to be absolutely that.

Sorting out Joan's house was a mammoth undertaking and I don't think I realized the true scale of what needed to be done until I got into it and was well on my way. I was an organization of one, but the project involved everything that is usually handled by a sizeable team and design staff: architecture, engineering, interiors, exteriors, landscaping, caretaker's house, pool, pool house, wells, septic systems, and generators. It was a total gut job and it went on and on. I tend to be very decisive and move very quickly, and Joan was actually very good to work with. I asked her to tear out pages from interior design magazines of anything that appealed to her, so that I could understand what she had in mind for her new home. I'd then come up with proposals for her to look at—that was her one opportunity to make any changes—and work would start soon afterwards.

Whenever her schedule allowed (sometimes once a month, at other times once a week), Joan would travel from New York to see how things were going. This inevitably involved her arriving in a limo and wearing some outrageously expensive outfit, all in front of a full construction crew with whom I'd torn myself apart negotiating over every dollar. Eventually, I felt I had to say something. "Joan dearest," I ventured, "do you not own an ordinary cloth coat, or could you possibly arrive in something other than a limo and furs?" She was divine in response, understanding the situation perfectly and even offering at my suggestion to stop at Dunkin' Donuts on her way over during future visits so she could buy a few dozen donuts for the crew. It is amazing how such small gestures can create such productive good will. Especially when served with a smile by Joan Rivers.

She only got out of line with me a couple of times during the entire construction and decorating process. On one occasion, she bought a chandelier that aesthetically belonged no more to the house than to the moon, and then later on she said she didn't want the stone terrace I had planned for the back of the house. I knew that the terrace would be a great asset, as it would have 180-degree views and provide Joan with a fabulous entertaining space. She insisted that she just wanted the grass to run right up to the house. I explained that that wasn't really appropriate unless she was planning to open a golf resort. So she got the terrace, and later thanked me for ignoring her. She loved having cocktail and dinner parties there with her Connecticut friends and some regulars that would often travel up from New York for a fun weekend with Joan. The infamous crystal chandelier never made its appearance in Connecticut and we both shared a number of good laughs over both stories.

Twice I quit the project. Twice we kissed and made up. The bottom line was that she very much respected what I was doing and what she had seen take shape from Day One. We had also started to become very close and to trust one another. Whenever anyone in Joan's world asked a question about the house, she would simply say, "Ask Joe." One afternoon, we went shopping together for landscaping materials at a local (and notoriously expensive) nursery. As we were walking through the grounds, I spotted the most amazing weeping copper beech, one of my favorite trees. It was quite the largest I had ever seen outside of a formal setting. I asked one of the staff how much it was and nearly passed out at the price. Joan showed no reaction, instead asking where I would put it. "You've got 80 acres, Joan," I replied, "so I'm sure we can find a good spot."

Eventually everything was done and Joan had her beautiful country home. The evening she arrived for her first night's sleeping there was a very special occasion for both of us. Everything outside and inside the house was perfect: lighting, window treatments, music, scented candles, fires glowing in all five fireplaces, the smell of apple pie in the oven, her favorite Cool Whip in the freezer, cookies on the bedside tables, chocolates, and water carafes in each room, beds turned down since it was late and she was bringing guests from New York. I decided not to be there when she arrived, as I wanted her to be greeted by her house and the staff and walk around without being concerned about what she needed to say—or perhaps not say—in front of me. Of course, she was on the phone with me bare minutes after arriving. By this point I knew her pretty well and could tell that her response was totally genuine. It was great to hear the excitement in her voice. She could not understand why I was not there when she arrived. I explained why and her reply was very Joan. "You're f***ing nuts. I hope you know that."

I felt a great sense of achievement with the project, especially when we got the cover of the August 2003 issue of *Architectural Digest* and a lovely nine-page feature on both of us. Most important, Joan had the country home that she wanted and it was so comforting to see her enjoy it whenever she could. Every evening she was there I had to be there as well, along with her handful of loyal friends. The house particularly came into its own after dusk, with the beautiful accent lighting, the roaring fires, and the laughter of people enjoying themselves and helping to create a truly enchanting atmosphere. To sit in the living room after dinner with Rex Reed, Alan Shayne, Norman Sunshine, and Polly Bergen, to name just a few, was to experience true magic.

Joan loved to shop and was very sincere about supporting local tradesmen. I'd pick her up to go on a buying expedition and often she'd be fast asleep in the passenger seat before we'd even reached her front gate. She had an extraordinary capacity to take a nap here and there, no matter the situation. One year, just before Christmas, we went into Pergola, one of the finest stores in Litchfield County and a great favorite of Joan's, not least because she loved the merchandise selected by the two men that ran it. I noticed a fabulous set of metal branches, as I had always loved antiques that can be placed outside. I couldn't read the price as I didn't have my glasses with me, but Joan (who annoyingly didn't need glasses, despite being a good deal older than me) told me what it was. It was a ridiculous amount of money.

A few days later, Peter Stiglin—one of the owners of Pergola—phoned and said he had a delivery for me. I was a bit confused, telling him that I hadn't ordered anything, but he said, "Don't worry about it, because Joan Rivers has." Then it dawned on me that it must be the branches. At first I protested, saying that they were far too expensive to have as a gift, but Peter told me not to fret too much as Joan had done so much arm-twisting on him to get a good price that he was considering a visit to an orthopedic surgeon to recover. It was classic Joan.

Besides her daughter and grandson, Joan's greatest joy was to entertain friends in her home. Friends who could not make it to dinner were invited instead for breakfast (she called them the "B list") sometimes at their peril. To watch Joan trying to make scrambled eggs was worth any price, and I have never seen anyone destroy an English muffin in quite the way she did. She was no domestic goddess, but that never stopped or slowed her down. She was Joan Rivers and she gave as she lived—with great enthusiasm and a wisecrack for every situation. As for the copper beech tree that we saw in the nursery that day, it is now maturing and resplendent on my front lawn. Much to my surprise, it was delivered there three months after we had seen it, another present from Joan. I knew how expensive it must have been and mumbled something to that effect to her. It drew a typically caustic reply. "You should learn to accept gifts graciously," she barked, "and make sure that f***ing tree gets enough water because if it dies, you'll be next. Don't ever forget that I have friends in Vegas." And most important: "I love you and the house you created for me." Yes indeed, Joan Rivers was a piece of work and most certainly a force of nature.

OPPOSITE A 24-foot-tall weeping beech appeared one day on my front lawn. Who else would have the nerve? Who else would be that generous? Joan Rivers waited for me to be out of the country and decided on its location. OVERLEAF LEFT AND RIGHT Lady Nancy "Slim" Keith believed that any garden should be treated as you would a home, that each turn should offer a new and exciting experience, a visual delight—one of the many lessons I will never forget.

For the majority of my life, my most amazing and cherished friendships have been with great women. I adore women, love being in their company, and have always found them to be much more interesting than most men, more capable of holding a stimulating conversation, and often gifted with a considerably better sense of humor. My female friends have always appreciated laughter and all have been fabulous communicators. Even more wonderful for me is the awareness that so many of them took such joy in introducing me to other great women.

Mollie Parnis, the fashion designer, suggested that Nancy Kissinger and I should be friends. At one point, she asked me, "Do you know Nancy Kissinger?" I replied that I hadn't met her personally, but had often seen her at social events and noticed how attractive she was, and that she seemed to have such natural style and elegance. "Well, you two need to know each other," Mollie said. "You'll like each other very much." Mollie always said exactly what she thought. Diplomacy was not her forte. I love remembering the evening she came to dinner at my New York apartment and decided, as we were about to sit down at the table, to take off her silk jacket. Being the proper host, I took the jacket with the intention of hanging it up. "Keep it where I can see it," she yelled. "Over on that chair is just fine." It took me seconds to understand her reasoning. The jacket had the most wonderful Schlumberger brooch pinned to its collar and there was just no way she was going to let that valuable beauty out of her sight.

Even in the company of a few close friends, Mollie did not let anything distract her. She did not suffer fools well at all. Having dressed first ladies and many political celebrities was not a badge of honor for Mollie. It was work and she loved her work. On one afternoon, in her showroom on Seventh Avenue, she was visited by the wife of a very well-known diplomat. The woman, I was told, behaved in a very condescending and grand manner. Of course, Mollie disliked her immediately. Whom the woman might be married to meant nothing to Mollie. After a few minutes, Mollie decided the woman had to go. "I don't believe we cut your size here, madame," she said, witheringly. If Mollie didn't like you, it was all over. So knowing how fond Mollie was of Nancy Kissinger was worth a good deal to me. To my good fortune, on one occasion in the early 1980s, I was invited to a dinner hosted by Edward and Myra Finkelstein at their country estate in Connecticut. Henry and Nancy Kissinger were on the guest list, with Henry recently appointed by Ed (the CEO of Macy's) to the department store's board of directors. There are few people who understand the cultures, governments, and politics of the world as Henry does. To this day, he is as brilliant as ever and as brilliant as they come. As an historian and a statesman, his views on what is going on around us are always bound to be compelling and insightful and sought-after by many world leaders. I thought his last book, *World Order*, published in 2014, was so well done that after reading it, I ordered the CDs, so that I could listen carefully and pick up everything and anything I might have missed by reading the book on my own. His understanding of the histories of the Soviet Union and China, in particular, is a revelation. He is the last of a kind, and it has always been a mesmerizing experience for me to be in his company, and listen when he talks about current affairs, or just

OPPOSITE My all-time favorite flower has always been the peony. There is just something very free and beautiful about peonies that lift one's heart. Now, I have three wonderful beds in my garden that bring forth hundreds of flowers each year, constantly reminding me how blessed I am to have friends in my life as special as Nancy Kissinger.

self-taught gardener,
and never happier than
when out digging, pruning,
and nurturing her
wonderful gardens with
their loyal dog, Abigail.

about any important subject of the day that should come up. I always seem to walk away from his company feeling that much smarter and more stimulated. And yes, incredibly lucky to have shared the same oxygen in his and Nancy's company.

Much to my delight, the Kissingers had accepted the Finkelsteins' dinner invitation. During cocktails, I remembered what Mollie had said, and, when I felt it was appropriate, I went up to Nancy Kissinger and introduced myself. I had always admired her from afar. So tall and statuesque, always dressed impeccably, and with her hair at just the perfect length. We talked for a while on a number of subjects. Since we live in very close proximity in the country, we quickly realized that besides world affairs we also shared many of the same local interests. Nancy has always been an advocate of land preservation and adores animals, especially dogs, as I do. I found her just as delightful and down to earth as I had imagined her to be and Mollie had always said she was. That conversation marked the start of a wonderful friendship. Henry traveled extensively, as one might expect, and Nancy very much enjoyed spending time at their country home and in the gardens she has created in rural Connecticut. I always look forward to the dinners she hosts, especially the intimate and informal occasions for just two or four people. When Henry is at home, the dinners are just as relaxed, and even when there are more guests, Nancy somehow manages to accommodate everyone at a large round table, so that all can join in the conversation. Henry always makes a toast of welcome, paying special tribute to Nancy and how much she means to him and their entire family and, of course, to those of us lucky enough to be considered their friends.

Nancy is a passionate, self-taught gardener, and never happier than when out digging, pruning, and nurturing her wonderful gardens with their loyal dog, Abigail. Thanks to Nancy, I now have the most beautiful peonies in my garden. They are the result of a phone call one morning from her asking me if I liked peonies. They are my favorite flower, I replied. "Good," she said, "I'm bringing some over." Nancy knows when to dig up the tubers of each plant and thin them out so there is room for future growth, and often shares the fruits of her labors with me. So much so that her gift of the original peonies has now multiplied to many dozens of individual plants. I have deliberately mixed the colors so that every summer I am surprised by the assortment in each bed. Nancy's peonies are a source of ongoing joy for me and my guests.

I had seen Brooke Hayward and her former husband, the bandleader Peter Duchin, often at many New York black-tie events, but had no relationship with either of them. Then one day I was sitting at Slim Keith's bedside having a pleasant afternoon visit during one of the many times her doctor ordered her to bed rest due to a recurring situation with heart disease. As we talked and laughed, the phone rang—it was Brooke, for Slim. They spoke for a short time and then Slim did something I absolutely hate; she handed me the phone and said, "Say hello to my stepdaughter Brooke." I'm not a big phone person to start with, and to talk to someone I didn't even know was not in my shy nature. But that was our introduction.

Slim became Brooke's stepmother when she married Leland Hayward in 1949. Brooke was only 12 years old when her new stepmother arrived on the scene and, while growing up in the entertainment business had to be a unique experience, I still cannot imagine what it must have been like having Slim introduced as your new mom. Since the friendship between Brooke and Slim lasted a lifetime, it was clearly a successful and comfortable relationship. Knowing both personalities as I now do, there was no question that they truly adored each other. In many ways, Brooke was a younger Slim. There were 20 years between them yet they had so much in common—wonderful looks, great taste, intelligence, and strong interests in anything creative and upbeat, and, of course, those great smiles and a divine sense of humor.

Although she grew up with two very well-known celebrity parents in the entertainment community, not all of Brooke's early life was as one would have thought. Her actress mother, Margaret Sullivan, died young, only to be followed in the same year by Brooke's sister, Bridget. The years that followed also brought the sadness of her brother Bill's passing. One of the reasons I adore and respect Brooke so much is how she handled such tragedy. She has never faltered in her integrity of being a positive spirit. Her lovely smile still lights up the room. Her command of the English language and intelligence became the tools that she drew upon to write the *New York Times* bestseller *Haywire* (which was made into a Hollywood movie in 1980).

Some of my fondest memories are of going over to Brooke's house for one of her lovely dinners. They were almost always held in the kitchen, overlooking a very dramatic garden and an amazing waterfall. There were wonderful and creative objects all around—even on the ceiling. All of a sudden you would notice, way up high on a wall, a collection of papier mâché masks. Or hanging from a rafter, three life-sized wood-carved birds, as though they had just settled there for a rest. I always felt I was in a shop of curiosities.

I had often admired what I felt was a most divine metal wreath hanging on Brooke's front door. Where in the world did she find it? One needs the gift of a certain eye and a level of creative confidence to be able to focus on such things. Brooke's wonderful wreath is now hanging by my front door. She just appeared one day for lunch with a big lovely smile on her face and the wreath in her hand. It had only taken me about 15 years of extended compliments.

PREVIOUS PAGES A 19th century French garden statue that greets guests at the entrance to our home was named George by my son, Christopher. In the winter, Chris would often try to keep George a bit warmer with a neck scarf on snowy days. OPPOSITE When Brooke Hayward Duchin arrived one day for lunch, she had a wonderful antique wreath with her. "Finally," I thought. It took about 15 years of admiring it at her home for it to make the trip to mine.

Brooke's wonderful wreath is now hanging by my front door. She appeared one day for lunch with a big lovely smile on her face and the wreath in her hand.

OPPOSITE Brooke Hayward Duchin adored her traveling companions, Oscar, Ike, and Lulu. When she would come to Connecticut for weekends, the parrots would always be with her. She had their travel needs down to a science.

THE HOUSE

OVERLEAF Many people don't expect to visit a house with a dark foyer, unless you are a friend of mine. I love a home with bits of drama here and there. The color is really not black but a secret formula I worked out years ago.

Bruce Binder was the older brother I always wished I had. He was a very genuine and caring person, always checking in with his friends to see if they were okay. His mother died when he was about 10 years old, and his father was never particularly supportive, so Bruce was basically raised by his mother's sisters, two wonderful aunts. I always felt that Bruce wanted nothing more than to be part of a family and had set about constructing one with his network of friends. He was a charming and attractive character, so that came easily. I always found it remarkable that he had a law degree, as he seemed to be the most unlawyer-like person.

Bruce was very imaginative and great at reinventing aspects of his life and past. He would often forget that he was just a Jewish kid from a middle-class family in the Bronx. That was mainly to do with the fact that he lived and worked in Paris for over 14 years as Macy's director of men's European fashion. The entire French thing seemed to overpower the Jewish dimension, and I believe that he actually thought he was French. For example, he could always get a reservation at any top Parisian restaurant by speaking on the telephone in his idiosyncratic Jewish style of French, sounding very grand and sometimes pretending to be a well-known doctor in Paris who had the same surname but sounded very different. The audacity of it made me laugh every time, and somehow it always seemed to work.

Heading to New York, we would often go to the airport in Paris together. Bruce would ask me to wait a minute while he had the most theatrical of conversations, convincing the people at the desk that he was important enough to be upgraded to first or business class. There was always plenty of French drama, and the result was that Bruce got upgraded and we were in the same cabin. Once seated next to me, he would proceed to bring out all sorts of goodies. He knew that I loved fresh figs, and, one time, had swung by Fauchon (one of the best gourmet stores in Paris) on his way to the airport to pick up figs and their amazing lemon cake for his friend Joey. Bruce was one of three people on the planet I let call me Joey.

Highly sociable, Bruce could work a room like a politician and used his great sense of humor to always find a laugh in a difficult situation. He was a consummate master of the art of exaggeration for dramatic effect, and I remember how, at Macy's, we had been hearing for years from Bruce about his swanky Parisian apartment with its view of the Eiffel Tower. Once, when I was in Paris with a group of high-ranking Macy's executives, Bruce offered to host a cocktail party. I couldn't wait to see his celebrated view of the Eiffel Tower and so, almost on arrival, I started prowling around from window to window looking for it. But none of them offered a view of Paris' most famous landmark. "Where is it then, Bruce?" I inquired. "Well," came the reply, "if I look out of this window and stretch a bit and look right across to your far right, you can just see it there." Clearly, advanced acrobatic skills were required, so I told Bruce to send me a postcard of the tower instead. It was a quintessential Bruce moment.

Bruce was well into his 40s when I started to become concerned about his financial future. While he had a good life in France, he never gave much thought to investing or to what the future might bring and how he might guarantee his security in old age. One day, I told him that I thought it was time he consider coming back to the United States to live and hopefully

OPPOSITE The 18th-century painting by Georges Michel was a house gift to Bruce Binder from a dear friend who had an amazing art collection. Bruce knew how much I admired it and, much to my surprise, left it to me in his will.

advance his career, and of course, make more money. I was also thinking about how much fun it would be to have Bruce back in New York. So I started work on my project to get Bruce back, enlisting the support of the people I needed to make it happen. This was in the early 1980s, when Macy's was opening stores across the country and key people were needed to fill new positions in the corporate offices in New York. As a result, some executive changes were made in the East Coast division and Bruce was back as a fashion director. He was so happy and excited. He immediately bought an apartment on East 57th Street and was busy telling the world that it was Bill Blass' building. I used to tease him often about this and remind him that Bill Blass did not actually own the whole building, just the penthouse.

Meanwhile, on one of those terribly hot New York days, as I was walking along Madison Avenue, I decided I needed to cool off for a minute or two before my next meeting. I happened to be passing by the air-conditioned sales office of a new building under construction and so I went in, pretending to be a potential buyer. I was so impressed with the plans of the different units that I walked out having just purchased a new apartment! Meanwhile, as soon as I got back to the office, I called Bruce and told him what I had just done and urged him to buy one of the apartments, too. He thought I was nuts. I set about convincing him that, as he liked to run in the mornings, it was a much better location than where he was because he would be right on Central Park. We figured out how to make it happen. Bruce could not have been happier with his new digs. It was a typical new New York City construction, with no detailing or decorative features. It did, however, have nine-foot-high ceilings, real plaster walls, and the best feature of all, eight-foot-high doors. Bruce got his famous friend, the French decorator, Jacques Grange, to help him with the apartment. Grange designed trompe l'oeil painted moldings around the ceilings and on the paneling of the doors, selected exquisite French tapestry fabric for the windows, and brought in a divine sofa covered in a stunning red Rubelli fabric. Ken Kocher, a good friend of Bruce's and a respected art collector, gave him a wonderful painting by the French artist Georges Michel as a housewarming gift, entitled *Landscape with Horse and Cart*. Bruce was over the moon. He had me down in his apartment the minute the painting arrived to help decide where it should go.

One day in the summer of 1992, Bruce mentioned that he was ready to take "the test for HIV." Then came that terrible day when Bruce called and asked if he could come and see me. He came into my office, closed the door, and sat in front of my desk. He then told me the results were positive. My blood ran cold, but all I could think of was to not let him see my reaction. I made light of the diagnosis since he appeared so healthy and suggested he have the test taken a second time on the grounds that mistakes were often made. He agreed that taking a second test was the right way forward and that's what he did. But it was positive, too.

Bruce fell progressively ill and passed away about five months later, in January of 1993. A short while later, his executor called me and said that Bruce had left me the Georges Michel painting in his will, along with his Jacques Grange red sofa. He knew I loved both, but we had never talked about such things and it was not something I could have anticipated. I was deeply touched. Now, every time I walk through my entrance hall, he is there, as I glance over to his painting. When I sit on the red sofa in my bedroom, as I often do with my dogs, Bruce is there, too. I will always be grateful for that.

ABOVE This photograph was taken when Bruce Binder was living in Paris as Macy's European fashion director. He looked the part and had the endearing personality that brought many European design houses to 34th street.

There is a better-than-average chance that this book would have turned out very differently if not for Ann Schmidt. It was Ann, my personal investigative reporter, who actually found this house for Chris and me while we were looking for a temporary rental. We were in between houses and I decided that I was not made for a rental and should buy something small and inexpensive. Out of frustration, I finally came to the realization that it would be a much better investment than paying rent every month and having no equity to show for it. After years of transforming many homes, I was confident that I had the creative vision and talent to make any house investment financially rewarding. I could also always hear my father saying: "You never rent, you own."

So I shared my thoughts with Ann one weekend and the next thing I knew, Chris and I had a house that we had planned to live in for only about two years while I built my dream home nearby. That was 18 years ago. Granted, it was a much smaller house back then, with absolutely no landscaping, stone walls, or pool. It now has tripled in size and enjoys a park-like setting. As they say, "If you want to make God laugh—tell Him your plans."

When I first moved to Litchfield County, I had purchased *Firefly*, the country home of Nancy "Slim" Keith. Once we got to know each other well, she told me that I must use a particular talent in the area who was gifted in the kitchen for lunches and dinners. Of course, I did whatever Slim directed and quickly engaged the wonderful Agnes Fairclough each and every time I planned to have guests. Before Slim, the house had belonged to Fredric March. It was the perfect country home in which to entertain. Once Slim got her hands on it, the house became magical. But the garden, designed by Florence Aldridge, was just not to be believed. Slim once told me that a garden should be treated just like the interiors of a beautiful home: It should be a delightful visual experience. Well, Aldridge surely had the same philosophy, and accomplished beauty at every turn in the 30-acre picture-book setting.

Much to my good fortune, not only did Agnes always do an excellent job, she also had a close friend who would always work with her at these events. It did not take long to understand that Ann was the operations manager in the partnership. And much to my delight, I noticed she was not only a very capable cook but was also amazing with my pet dogs. Since I had four at the time, they were the perfect test of Ann's true love of animals.

Soon, I found myself looking for someone to take care of my country home when I was in New York or traveling, which was often. I wanted very much to ask Ann if she would be interested but was apprehensive about insulting her in any way. So I did what every good New Yorker would do: I simply asked her if she could possibly recommend anyone. Thank God she quickly made me understand that she would be interested herself, and now the rest is history. That was almost 40 years ago. The years seemed to move very quickly and there is no question that Ann became a most valued friend and member of our little family. Even after she retired, she was always with us.

She was there for Christopher and me from his first visit to Connecticut. On weekends, once Chris was old enough not to have to travel with a nanny, Ann would come stay with us on

OPPOSITE Some of the antique English porcupine-quill boxes I like to display in the entrance foyer on a Louis Philippe étagère cost thousands of dollars apiece. Ann Schmidt found the one she gave me for 50 cents at a tag sale.

weekends and plan outings and play dates for Chris that I would have never been able to arrange on my own. She is very well read and just knew about every event in the county that a child of his age would want to be part of. She would drive Christopher from event to event with the most delightfully positive energy and caring attitude. Being used to my way of driving, Chris found Ann's driving a bit slow and wasted little time in making his thoughts known to her. I guess this occurred once too often for Ann's good nature, for finally very near our home, she stopped her car and suggested Chris get out and walk since he was so critical and ungrateful. Christopher could spend eight hours on the basketball court and never complain, but ask him to walk a city block and he perceived it as sheer torture. He never complained to Ann again after that day. They went everywhere together on those weekends. And much to my surprise, one of Christopher's very favorite things to do was to stop at tag sales. Ann would act as his banker and he had great fun finding that special something that always seemed to make his day.

I always found it interesting that Ann, one of the most unmaterialistic people on the planet, was drawn to tag sales. As a result, her friends have become the beneficiaries of her one small indulgence. She has brought so many wonderful treasures to our home that you can be sure cost her next to nothing. For one dollar, she found the William Paley special edition birthday book done by his family. A friend found one a short time after in an antique bookstore and actually paid $500. Why? I will never understand, although it does have some very special photographs in it that have never been published before or since. Ann also found an old issue of Andy Warhol's *Interview* with Joan Rivers on the cover. Of course she had to buy it for me, knowing my close relationship with Joan. And it was just one dollar. Meanwhile, many years ago, I started a collection of antique porcupine-quill boxes when traveling on business in England. I always thought them to be very decorative but unless I was lucky when on the hunt, they were also very overpriced. One afternoon, Ann arrived with one she found in perfect condition at a tag sale for 50 cents. I could not believe my eyes. In addition to all her other attributes, she has a very good eye.

Ann is a very special friend—perhaps my most cherished. Her love and genuine caring are unique, and her faith and sense of life values are inspirational. Yes, yet another amazing woman who has blessed my life, and with God's grace, will continue to do so.

OPPOSITE Ann Schmidt and Christopher were photographed one Saturday morning setting out on an adventure to a baseball game or tag sale. They adored each other, although Chris complained that Ann didn't drive as fast as Dad.

Whenever I think of David Leong, I think of sunshine, because when he walked into a room, the place somehow lit up. Never overbearing or imposing in any way, his wonderful smile and sparkling eyes immediately made you aware of his presence. He also had the enviable gift of making people feel comfortable around him, even those with whom he might not immediately have much in common.

I remember the June day in 1976 when David first walked into my office at Macy's wearing a wonderful apple-green jacket and a pair of black designer pants. Little did I know at the time that not only were the pants and jacket his own designs, but that he had actually hand-made the garments himself. And yet he was not there to talk about his apparel but to discuss his luggage designs.

At that time, the Macy's luggage department had boring products. Luggage was black, grey, or tan for the most part, and the department looked just like every other luggage store across the country. However, the Macy's buyer was enthusiastic, high-energy, and just needed a push from a partner in management to try something new and different. I had learned years before how important it was to give merchants the reassuring sense that any risk they might consider taking would be in partnership with someone higher up. What that did was give the young merchant someone with whom they could share the possible disappointment and sense of failure if things did not work out. In this case that person was me. I always loved thinking out of the box. And for me, there was no better partner in retailing than an enthusiastic merchant to be taken where no man had gone before.

The luggage buyer at the time was Gail Jarvis, who seemed to have all the qualities required to make special things happen. So when I walked the floor with her one morning and asked how we could bring distinctiveness, creativity, and color to this drab and boring department, she said, "Just give me a little time and I'll get back to you." A couple of days later, she came into my office with a copy of an article in *New York* that featured a young designer who was experimenting with quilted microfiber fabrics in a variety of colors and shapes that were unusual for that time. To emphasize his design direction, he had also come up with matching thermal suits for cold weather travel. It was all straight out of a James Bond movie, as unique as it was fabulous. What I found particularly exciting was that there was nothing else like it on the market then, anywhere. I always loved making Macy's first.

"Let's go and see him immediately," I said to Gail. She came back shortly afterwards, looking very disappointed. Apparently this extremely creative designer was a one-man show that would never be able to supply the volume that a Macy's order would entail. He had no capital, no showroom, and no office, and made every piece himself in the rented, unheated loft space in which he both lived and worked. I recall hearing that he did not even have hot water. Gail said that she would keep looking for someone else, but I pointed out that there is always more than one way to skin a cat and that we should meet this guy anyway. At the appointed hour, Gail walked in my office with Mr. Sunshine: David Leong. Within seconds, it was apparent how enormously creative this young designer was. I remember

OPPOSITE David Leong's gift of these antique leather-bound books became the perfect background on the table in the foyer for the antique English brass letters I had found at the Bermondsey Market in London—a must-visit.

thinking that he possessed such a unique and positive spirit. The three of us talked for some time, worked out collection opportunities, and eventually Gail and I decided that David's creativity and sincerity were worth the risk. We arranged for Macy's to provide him with some minimal pre-financing, so that he could purchase the materials required to manufacture the styles we wanted. He then proceeded to work day and night to create the products that would get him onto Macy's highly coveted stage. I'm not going to say that we ultimately sold many thermal suits, but that was never our intention. But it was the thermal suits, through David's creativity and Macy's effective mechandising presentation, that were the traffic stoppers that made everyone's efforts a business success. We did, however, sell out several times over on the microfiber quilted bags. *That* was our intention. Little by little, other stores discovered David at Macy's and his name became known. He was always ahead of his time in terms of his design ideas.

Soon afterwards, David called me and invited me to dinner. It did not take long for me to realize how special he was, and that dinner marked the start of one of the most cherished relationships of my life. David and I were the best of friends for 15 years, during which time we spent all our free time together. We came from very different mindsets in terms of what was important in the greater scheme of things. His priority was the appreciation of all the good things in life, whereas for me, my career took priority over everything. Personal relationships were in decidedly second place. Looking back, as I have all too often since, I see that David was right and I was wrong.

I am not sure where David is today and wish that I did. Still, he remains with me through some of the lovely gifts that he gave me over the years, most notably the antique jade coin he brought back for me from his first visit to Hong Kong. The antique leather-bound books that grace the round center table in my entrance hall are another reminder of David's generosity. I wish he could see them there, with the old English brass letters spelling out "CICIO" to all the guests I welcome into my home—just in case they are unsure they've come to the right place! David's books hold a place of honor and serve as a constant reminder of the warm and cherished times we shared.

OPPOSITE When David Leong worked for two months in Hong Kong designing sportswear, it was the first time we were apart since we became friends. He brought this antique jade Chinese coin back for me. I instantly loved it.

The antique leather-bound books that grace the round center table in my entrance hall are another reminder of David's generosity. I wish he could see them there, with the old English brass letters spelling out "CICIO" to all the guests I welcome into my home.

OPPOSITE David Leong, the fashion and luggage designer, had a fine eye and an appreciation for beautiful things.

In the fall of 1975, I went to Macy's for a series of interviews for a position as the store's new administrator for visual merchandising. This process was initiated by Mike Stemen, and as a result he was the very first executive I met there. Mike was the Senior Vice-President and Director of all stores at that time. After several one-on-one interviews, Mike had me meet a host of other executives whom he wanted to consult on whether or not to offer me the position. I think he sensed early on I was hesitant about making the move from Fifth Avenue's Lord & Taylor to 34th Street's Macy's, but he was also smart enough to bring out some very heavy guns to help convince me, and they were comfortable that I would be a good fit. Few would remember how sad a store Macy's was back then. Though I was not entirely sold on a job relocation, Mike asked me to meet Mrs. G.G. Michelson, the Senior Vice-President of Human Resources at Macy's. Until Mike brought Mrs. Michelson into play, it was clear to him that this was becoming a difficult sell. He was also confident that I would be no match for one of the most impressive and respected women in the business at the time. So it was that, after a meeting lasting more than two hours—during which Mrs. Michelson and I sat together and had what was, for me, a fascinating conversation about retailing generally and Macy's in particular—I was left thinking, "How could I turn down the chance to work with people of this caliber?" Mike's plan had worked beautifully.

Mike and I went on to enjoy a very productive relationship at Macy's for many years. One of the many things I learned to admire about Mike was his positive attitude toward any challenge. Mike is that special person who seems to walk into one's life always seeing the glass half-full. There was just no challenge he would not take on for the betterment of the business. It was no small decision on the part of Mike and his wonderful wife, Karen, to make the dramatic move to New York from the lovely picture-book existence they enjoyed in San Francisco—and to accomplish such a complete lifestyle change with genuine grace and enthusiasm. I have noticed over the years that, for many people, moving from coast to coast— in either direction—can be a very difficult transition. But the changes in lifestyle, work habits, and daily priorities can be even more difficult. Many of those who attempt the move don't seem to last very long in their new location, but Mike and Karen just had everything required to make it a success. Even with all their family still back on the West Coast, they became Easterners almost instantly. But not, I should add, before their adventurous spirit guided them to live first on their boat from California that was docked at the marina on West 72nd Street, before they finally took an apartment at the Osborne on West 57th Street.

I have no idea how many times a day I would run down to Mike's office, soliciting his support to help accomplish my various goals. He handled each and every crisis with calm, reason, and usually a smile. In my very early days at Macy's, before I was able to build my own team, I felt rather overwhelmed, and with good reason. Mike was great at coping with this new and rather unusual creative spirit who seemed to think that everything was not only vitally important but also had to be fixed that same day. Thank God that we had developed

OPPOSITE The commissioned porcelain pillbox features portraits of my first dogs, Asta and Piper. Little did Mike and Karen Stemen know that their thoughtful gift would be the start of a fun collection. The first time I saw one of the *Thin Man* movies, I decided that I too, someday, would have a wire hair fox terrier. To date, I have had seven.

ABOVE On July 31, 1986, Mike and Karen Stemen attended the black-tie event at the Metropolitan Museum of Art in New York, celebrating Edward S. Finkelstein's achievement of taking Macy's private through a leveraged buyout.

early on a very honest and direct working relationship. It was no secret that there was always an unwritten rivalry between West Coast Macy's and East Coast Macy's. I remember once telling Mike how I was so tired of hearing him refer to how much better things were in Macy's California. So one day, when I had heard enough, I told him so. He looked at me, smiled, and said, "You're absolutely right, Joe. I'll agree to stop talking about Macy's California if you agree to quit telling me how wonderful it was at Lord & Taylor." Touché. As usual, he was right on target and I told him so with a big smile. Thereafter, we both kept our word to each other.

Mike and I accomplished so much together, and I feel confident that he would agree that it was more like productive fun than just a good deal of tireless work. We both not only believed in our mission; we both loved making it a reality. We built great teams that were totally dedicated to the job at hand and committed to Edward S. Finkelstein's vision for Macy's, and we helped develop a superb business with some of the most talented associates in retailing. For me, the joy of working with Mike was immeasurably enhanced by also getting to know his wife, Karen, always charming and supremely capable in her own right. And always with a wonderful smile. If they were not husband and wife they would have been brother and sister, I would often think. They were both blessed with a positive, "can do" spirit. I used to love the small dinner parties they would host, gatherings where great conversation was always guaranteed with just the right amount of laughter. Memories I especially treasure include a wonderful costume Halloween party they gave in a neighbor's empty apartment in their building, and also a tag sale we organized to help raise money for a lobby upgrade. They lived in one of the very grand older buildings of New York called the Osborne. When originally built in 1883, it was one of the most impressive buildings in New York. But like many buildings of that period, it had been neglected and needed repairs and upgrades. Not however with the Stemens in residence, and, of course, with Mike's take-charge abilities as president of the condominium board.

Mike and Karen have always been very thoughtful and giving individuals. There is just about nothing they would not do for a friend. Their extreme thoughtfulness was really brought home to me by a particular gift they gave me one Christmas. They knew (as did everyone at Macy's) of my love for wire hair fox terriers, and so they had commissioned for me a custom-painted Limoges box depicting my first two dogs, Asta and Piper. The thoughtfulness this gift represents has always touched me. Any of us could walk into a store and buy something lovely for a friend, but this was an entirely different level of giving. The box is now the centerpiece of a small wire-hair artifacts collection that sits on a small table. I pass it several times every day, and Mike and Karen invariably come to mind. I guess I must also admit that I am often reminded by the collection of Nick and Nora Charles of the famed *Thin Man*. When I was very young, I remember being mesmerized by one of the movies and this wonderful dog full of personality running about. It was the famous Asta, and I promised myself that one day, I would have such a dog. I could never have anticipated that the first dog for me would come out of the Macy's Children's Pet Department on the fifth floor—one more example of Ed Finkelstein's passion to make his store more entertaining.

OVERLEAF In planning any entertaining spaces in a home, I feel there should always be various options for easy conversation, a place to put down a drink, and a light to read a book. The spacious living room has many such areas.

I met Slim Keith because I decided to relocate my country residence after ten years in Wilton, Connecticut. I was determined to look for a weekend home further north, where I could find properties with more land and privacy. When I first moved to Wilton, it was the perfect location for me, in the country but only an hour's commute to New York. Litchfield County seemed to be a very good alternative, from what I had been told by friends like Oscar de la Renta and Bill Blass, both of whom had homes there. I have seen and owned enough homes to know in seconds whether or not a place is for me. I have always believed that with good taste and creativity, one can make just about anything look good.

I love bringing new life to a space. It can be a very rewarding experience emotionally, and of course it can also bring financial dividends if all the important elements are in place. On this particularly memorable day of house hunting, my realtor and I had visited a number of properties within my budget, but none had sparked any enthusiasm. Then we went to see a house called *Firefly*. It instantly reached out to me emotionally and aesthetically, but it was considerably over my budget (not usually a deterrent, as those who know me well will confirm).

Firefly was the quintessential Connecticut country property. Thirty acres of pure perfection. The drive up to the house ran between beautiful stone walls and over a lovely bridge amidst stunning mature landscaping, once the passion of Florence Aldridge, the wife of the celebrated actor Fredric March. The house was a 1740 saltbox, painted the most chic tone of muddy cocoa. Beautiful terra cotta-potted flowering plants (white only, of course) cascaded down the front door steps. It was magical. No one was home, so I could open every cabinet and closet and investigate at will. *Firefly* was put together in the most unpretentious way and with a great sense of style and taste. I was totally mesmerized, and asked who owned the house. She said it was a Lady Nancy Keith, and I remember saying, "I can tell you that whoever Lady Keith is, she is an amazing individual. Look at the pictures on the skirted table. Look at the pig on top of that Regency bookcase. Look at the little girl in a broad-striped beach towel in the photograph in the silver frame. Yes, Lady Keith is a very special personality."

Lady Keith had had that rare ability to put it all together and make it work, and I could tell that a decorator had not set foot in the place. Very few people can mix humor with both expensive and inexpensive things and end up with the result I had in front of me that day. I decided that I had to get to know this person. Yet, until I went back to the home of Macy's CEO Edward S. Finkelstein and his wife Myra for lunch that day, I still had no idea who Lady Keith was.

Of course, Ed knew exactly who she was and proceeded to tell me about her three husbands: Howard Hawks, the famous movie director, Leland Hayward, the famous theatrical agent and producer, and Lord Kenneth Keith, the famous English financier and young CEO of British Airways. It was an impressive pedigree. "But, no, Ed, I am not buying the house," I said. "I love it, but it is way over my budget and I can't afford to stretch that much for a weekend home." Ed insisted that we all go back that afternoon for a second look. He was much more interested in seeing Lady Keith than the house, as he was always very taken by celebrity. Much to my astonishment (and Ed's delight), the lady herself opened the door. I can still recall

OPPOSITE The ivory articulated crab, on a small table in the living room, was left to me in Slim Keith's will in 1990, with a note from her hidden inside it. The photograph is of Slim and Howard Hawks on their honeymoon in 1941.

ABOVE Lady Nancy "Slim" Keith was one of the most beautiful women of her time. No wonder Howard Hawks married her.

every element of her appearance—from the French double-faced picot-edge silk ribbon in her hair to the espadrilles on her feet. She was statuesque, with the best posture and a very captivating and natural presence. On that landmark afternoon, Slim greeted us warmly. She invited us in and various introductions took place. We were a large group, due to the different realtors involved and the prospective buyer family of three (me and the Finkelsteins). "Please feel free to look around," she breezed. "Open all the closets. We are very neat here." Then, as though she were following a script from one of Leland Hayward's plays, she returned to the living room sofa in front of a blazing fire to continue reading her book.

Little did I know that my life would change in so many ways as a result of that visit. We toured the house, took in every room, and left politely. I absolutely adored it, but remained determined that I would not buy it because of the price. I tried to get it out of my mind and soon after went off to Europe on a business trip with some of my associates at Macy's. Somehow, we found ourselves with a free Sunday and decided to visit the country home of the Impressionist painter Claude Monet, at Giverny. Well, that was either the end or the beginning of it all. It was the most beautiful country home I had ever seen and suddenly all I could think of again was *Firefly* and the possibility of it being my own.

Shortly after returning to New York, I went to the ballet with the Finkelsteins. During the performance, Ed nudged me and said, "Look who's sitting over there." It was Slim Keith, with Oscar de la Renta, Annette Reed, and John Richardson. Ed was determined to make contact during the Intermission. Being very shy, I am not good in crowds, but before I knew it, we had exchanged greetings with Slim and returned to our seats. I could neither take my eyes off her nor stop thinking about *Firefly*. So I decided that the house budget would somehow work itself out, and I started negotiating for the house that week. I got the price down by 20 percent and was able to buy a few of the beautiful antiques from Slim directly.

Even before the house purchase was concluded, Slim and I had started to develop a very meaningful friendship. It was no secret that Slim loved men and, as much as I was basically very shy, I was totally captivated by her. Being with her was almost like stepping into a movie. She and I were to go on and share many wonderful evenings, weekends, and memorable times together until her death four years later in 1990. We talked on the phone, often three or four times every day. I used to love making her laugh. She once told me, early on, that, now that we were such good friends, she was a little disappointed that "those little velvet boxes" had not yet started to arrive at her home. She was referring to the Hollywood days when jewels were lavished on those who were loved. Macy's had just purchased I. Magnin in California, which sold very expensive faux jewelry in its Los Angeles store. So I started buying Slim wonderful faux diamond bracelets, earrings, and rings, which even with my Macy's employee discount, I could barely afford. One night we had dinner with her dear friend William Paley, the founder of CBS, who could not take his eyes off what looked like a 15-carat diamond ring that Slim adored flashing. Eventually, he said, "Slim, I think that after all these years I know most of your exquisite jewelry, but that ring is new to me. Where did it come from?" "Oh, this one, Billy? Just a recent interest," she beamed, fluttering her eyelashes. The interest was seated on Slim's left at that very table.

Slim had it all. Beauty, intelligence, and taste, plus a well-read knowledge of just about every subject from food, to religion and politics, to medicine. The first 50 years or so of Slim's amazing life were filled with people and events that most of us only read about. She experienced so much, mixing with the most fashionable celebrities of the day and always being invited to the most stylish parties. It all kind of started with a road trip she took at the age of 18 across the Mojave Desert in a convertible. She wrote in her autobiography about how she was wearing a powder-blue wool suit and matching felt hat "with a jaunty flower on the side." She ended up at the Furnace Creek Inn, where she met leading Hollywood stars Warner Baxter and William Powell next to the swimming pool. She was soon part of a glittering circle that saw her mixing with the likes of Cary Grant and William Randolph Hearst. She was a regular visitor to Hearst Castle in San Simeon on the California coast.

Years later, I was traveling from San Francisco to Los Angeles and stopped off at Hearst Castle, never having been there before. By then, it was a national historic landmark and no longer owned by the Hearst family. Slim called me that evening in my hotel room. "So honey, what did you think of it all?" she asked. The truth was that I was very unimpressed with what I had seen, taste not being a key ingredient as far as I was concerned. Two things did amaze me, however. First, the scale of what Hearst had achieved in the execution of his vision for the place, and second, the Grecian swimming pool, which I found a total fantasy and beautifully done. "Oh yes," said Slim, "I spent many a wonderful afternoon sunbathing next to that pool." One can only imagine who else was there with her, as the castle was regularly filled with the good, the great, and the most fashionable.

At various stages in her life, Slim was great friends with Ernest Hemingway, often visiting him in Cuba, and Truman Capote, who called her "Big Mama" (although they were later to fall out irrevocably). One of Slim's greatest finds was Lauren Bacall, whom she told her husband Howard Hawks to cast in a movie. As a result, 'Betty' Bacall became not only a huge Hollywood star but also one of Slim's closest friends. They were like peas in the proverbial pod, so similar in look, voice, dress, and movement that at times it was uncanny.

Slim never failed to have an impact wherever she went. I recall how one evening a group of us were having dinner at Don Hewitt's apartment on Central Park South in Manhattan. We were all in the living room enjoying cocktails when, all of a sudden, the fabulous and very smart fashion designer Mollie Parnis walked through, yelling across the room, "Slim, I am never going to a dinner party again that you're at!" "For heaven's sake, why not, Mollie?" asked Slim. "Because every man in the place is around you, hanging on your every word," came the reply. "It is simply not fair."

For all her charm and personality, Slim could also be very insecure and, as a result, even a little vulnerable. For me this made her even more perfect, if that were possible. She had seen so much, to the point that when her health started to fail she appeared to care little about living much longer. She smoked far too much, but knew that this upset me and so when she was expecting me to visit, she would always try to hide the cigarettes—usually in the woodpile next to the drawing-room fireplace—and would burn scented candles to mask

OPPOSITE Only Slim Keith's amazing eye could have found this rare brass bird—one of a pair—in an outdoor market in Turkey. When she gave them both to me, many years later, she made me promise never to polish them.

the smell of tobacco. She used to give the doorman in her building $20 to go and buy cigarettes for her (which then cost about $2 a pack), but he would always tell me what was going on and you could smell the scented candles as soon as you got in the elevator.

Slim had a tremendous sense of humor, right to the end. Late one evening, I switched on the television to catch Charlie Rose on his chat show, in case he had an interesting guest. Slim and I both admired Charlie and his show, and on this occasion I was fascinated to see Pamela Harriman being interviewed. There she was in her Chanel suit and with a Hermès bag, looking very Pamela. There was no love lost between her and Slim, as Pamela had "stolen" Leland Hayward, Slim's one true love, away from her. "Wow," I thought, "do I dare dial Slim at this late hour to tell her to switch on the TV?" She was on my speed dial and, knowing that she was a bit of an insomniac, I thought, what the hell, just do it. She picked up the telephone and, before I even had a chance to say anything, growled, "I am watching every detail of every minute!" We watched the entire one-and-a-half hour program whilst on the phone together.

I am so grateful for the many cherished possessions in this house that remind me of her, none more so than an articulated ivory crab. One day, Slim called me at my office and said, "I want you to know that I've left you something totally divine in my will." I tried to stop the conversation, since I found it truly upsetting, but she insisted that I listen to her. Without revealing what the object was, she told me that when I would eventually receive it, I must look in the secret compartment on the side, in which I would find a note from her. Years later, on the day of her memorial, her daughter Kitty came to my apartment for lunch with this amazing crab in her hand. I remembered it immediately, since it was always in the center of Slim's dining-room mantelpiece. She had bought it when in London with her great friend Bill Blass, from the antiques dealer Mallett on Bond Street. Of course, I cried when I found the note.

One of my most treasured possessions is a 19th-century Meissen porcelain monkey once owned by Slim that I acquired under remarkable circumstances. About a month after she passed away, I went to a charity auction at Sotheby's in New York and saw the monkey. I had no idea at the time that it had belonged to Slim, but was mysteriously drawn to it. The auction was by silent bids and it was only when I looked at the bidding form that I saw that the monkey had been "in the ownership of Lady Keith." There was just one other bid, so I placed mine and carried on looking around. Every so often I would go back to see if I had any competition. Each time my only competitor had raised the bid, I increased mine. This went on seven times. The day before the actual auction, I got a call from John Rosselli, a well-known antiques dealer in New York. "Are you bidding on the monkey because you love it?" he asked, "or because it belonged to Slim Keith?" Of course I said I was interested in it because it had belonged to Slim and I was terribly depressed about her passing. "Then you should have it with my fondest wishes," he replied. "She was an amazing woman."

OPPOSITE This 19th century Meissen monkey was a gift from Slim Keith to a New York charity before she passed away. When I saw it was coming up at auction I had to have it. Thanks to John Rosselli, it is now in my living room. OVERLEAF LEFT The leopard-pattern Rubelli fabric moment by the window in the living room just seemed to happen. A passion for collecting helped in putting it together. OVERLEAF RIGHT French King Louis XVI's animal court painter's flair for the dramatic comes across in this painting. Slim Keith passed this treasure on to me for "safekeeping."

93

We all remember in *My Fair Lady* when Audrey Hepburn comes to the top of the stairs at 27 Wimpole Street in that beautiful white evening dress. Hair up high, with a glittering tiara and that amazing long neck with diamonds to spare. I sat in the theater in Brooklyn, New York, a young man in my early teens, watching *My Fair Lady*, and immediately fell in love. I clearly remember saying to myself back then, "Some day I will marry a girl that looks just like that." Little did I know that was never to be in the cards, but equally unknown to me then was that, many years later, Audrey Hepburn and I were destined to become friends.

Fast-forward more than a quarter of a century. I was enjoying a wonderfully exciting and enriching career in retail. In 1988, Macy's had purchased the San Francisco-based specialty store I. Magnin, the bespoke retailer on the West Coast that had unfortunately lost a good deal of its prestige and with it, the support of the high-end designer market. Within days of the purchase, Macy's corporate CEO Edward S. Finkelstein appointed Rosemarie Bravo as the new CEO of this now lackluster but former luxury retail icon. She was charged with turning I. Magnin's fortunes around, and as a result, all eyes in the industry were on her.

One very important element of the store's business was its renowned special events, held not only for the customers but also aimed at the designer trade. Aside from the need for special and distinctive merchandising, Rosemarie knew that these events were important tools in helping restore consumer and market confidence. The annual Valentine's Ball was one of the most important I. Magnin events, a black-tie dinner held under a tent on their rooftop with a designer runway fashion show in the store. Every year, a particular designer would be chosen to headline the Valentine's Ball, and in 1990, the store decided to honor the French fashion designer Hubert de Givenchy. In a stroke of genius, Rosemarie and her team came up with the wonderful idea of surprising Hubert with an unannounced personal appearance by one of his dearest friends, Audrey Hepburn.

That evening was one of the most beautiful and moving events I had ever experienced in the fashion business. Toward the end of the runway show, Hubert had walked to the front of the runway as planned and was completely oblivious as to what was about to happen, even when the models quickly exited on cue and the music was replaced by *Moon River*. Suddenly Audrey appeared at the opposite end of the runway—breathtaking and most captivating in a long, cream-colored Givenchy evening dress, holding a matching bouquet of exquisite French tulips. Still unaware of who was standing on the stage behind him, Hubert turned to exit the runway and there she was. It was a magical moment, as a smile of delighted recognition lit up his face. Audrey presented Hubert with the tulips and the two dear friends embraced affectionately. There was not a dry eye in the house. Of course it helps if you are an Audrey Hepburn fan.

At the end of that magical evening, Macy's had planned to fly Audrey and her companion Robert Wolders back to Los Angeles on the company Gulfstream Jet. I was one of the seven passengers on board. Except that this was far from pure chance. Ed knew how much I adored Audrey from afar and had invited me to join them on the return flight. That was more than I could have ever fantasied. I can recall every detail of Audrey's traveling outfit, from her Ferragamo shoes to her Loro Piana turtleneck sweater. Ed's wife Myra, who was sitting next to Audrey,

OPPOSITE Audrey Hepburn surprised fashion designer Hubert de Givenchy at the I. Magnin Valentine's Ball in 1990.

insisted I swap seats with her so that I could talk to Audrey one on one. With that gesture, I was able to meet my idol properly. We discovered that we had many common interests. And so started a friendship. Audrey and I kept in regular contact and she would on occasion visit me in New York. Once, when she came for dinner, she brought a collection of rag dolls made by UNICEF children in the national costumes of eight countries in which the charity was active. Audrey was passionate about doing whatever she could to help children in the developing world, and she worked tirelessly to raise awareness for UNICEF by visiting many different countries and bringing firsthand attention to the educational and medical needs of children living in poverty. The rag dolls were for my son Christopher, who was less then two years old at the time. We still have them.

While I was at Macy's, Audrey accepted my invitation to design her dream room as part of the "celebrity room" series I had created for our antiques department—to promote the business and create more traffic. When I look back to that time, I am honestly surprised I had the courage to also ask Audrey to appear in person for a ribbon cutting as we opened her room to the public. But I had and I did. The response from the public that she was coming to Macy's was remarkable. We had never seen such crowds. As always, the store's security department did an outstanding job, with an estimated 8,000 people coming to The Corner Shop to see Audrey in person. Before she cut the ribbon, Audrey addressed the audience, explaining how she envisioned the perfect kitchen as a room where the whole family could gather together, with a stone fireplace, a big country table, blue-and-white china, upholstery and a desk with a computer where, she said, "Dad can work while still being with the family."

The event was a huge success and I was over the moon about Audrey's response to it. As a thank you, she sent me a delightful folk-style painting of a girl holding a doll, which she had found in a very small shop in Switzerland. She adored it since it also reminded her of the gift of dolls she had given to Christopher a few months before. She was also concerned, she told me, about whether I would like the painting, and feel that it would fit in our home. How could I not? She had picked it out especially for us. With the painting came a note saying how perfectly executed the room in Macy's had been and that it was totally in tune with her own vision, right down to the wooden bowl of walnuts on the center table: "My favorite evening treat," she confessed. She wondered how I knew that. I confessed I didn't, but often have a bowl of walnuts on the table of my country kitchen as well. We just laughed.

Audrey was hugely creative, and when she wrote to friends she would often do a small drawing on the front of the cards. Knowing that she cared enough to do this makes them very special to me and to all the others who received them. I have been priviledged to know many celebrities. These encounters were always interesting and often very enjoyable. Yes, on a few occasions they could be a little disappointing, but to this day no one has ever come close to Audrey's loveliness. She was one of those rare celebrities who was the same person through and through. Genuine and dedicated to doing well for others, Audrey was not just a cherished friend, she was also an angel of our time. Like so many, I adored her.

OPPOSITE This small painting was a gift from Audrey Hepburn that could not be more indicative of her true and honest spirit—understated and sweet, with absolutely no pretense. Regrettably, she never did get to see it framed.

Retailing, fashion merchandising, and interior design are the industries in which I was fortunate enough to forge an exciting career. These worlds attract a very diverse collection of talents—dedicated and dynamic innovators who give hugely of their time, energy, creativity, passions, and accomplishments. Josie Natori and her husband Ken have built one of the most successful businesses in an ever-challenging fashion landscape. The Natori Company has become a respected international brand purely because of their talent, hard work, and dedication to their dream. The Natori business began with very special hand-embroidered lingerie, but then expanded into one fashion category after another, reaching the couture-level apparel now offered at some of the finest retailers internationally.

I first met Josie and Ken while at Macy's, probably when we were in the process of renovating the second-floor lingerie department at the Herald Square store in the late 1970s. Over the years, I have shared many wonderful experiences with the Natori family all over the world—from Manila, to Paris, where Christopher ate prawns for the first time in a small bistro. I also learned that Robert DeGaetano, the pianist and composer, had a house in Harlem, where he had two concert grand pianos facing each other: one for the student and the other for the teacher. Of course, the pianos had to be Steinways. I would never have developed a relationship with Robert were it not for Josie and Ken, and sadly remember crying years later at Robert's memorial, which Josie orchestrated to perfection. Josie is a highly accomplished pianist as well. Could any of us fortunate enough to be befriended by the Natoris ever forget the evening they took over Carnegie Hall to celebrate a special birthday of Josie's? She performed on stage for all their friends, playing Rachmaninoff! There were over 1500 guests at the concert, and Christopher and I were privileged to be seated in the front row. What amazing confidence and talent she had, to be able to perform on one of the most famous stages in musical history. When Christopher showed his own interest in taking piano lessons, I called Josie to see if she could recommend a good teacher. A few months later, Josie and Ken came for dinner and wanted to hear Christopher play. Josie took me aside and said she felt that Christopher had great potential, but that I must get rid of that piece of junk in my living room and replace it with a Steinway. I looked at her and told her I had just spent a small fortune refurbishing that piece of junk. Josie insisted it had to go. Christopher deserved better, and furthermore Robert would take over the lessons. I now have a Steinway grand in my living room that is so much more than just a beautiful piano. It never fails to bring Josie, Robert, and Christopher to mind each and every time I look at it.

Josie and Ken are seldom out of my mind when I walk through my house. The beautiful gifts they've given me over the years—the malachite glass vase now on Christopher's Steinway, or perhaps the Tang horse or the miniature Chinese lions—they all bring Josie and Ken back to me at every turn. All carry very special memories and are a reminder that the objects that surround us will always do their job if we are open to the positive message they deliver and the memories they bring back.

OPPOSITE The Tang Dynasty decanter and the malachite vase, which both sit on the Steinway grand piano in the living room, were gifts from Josie and Ken Natori and are examples of the exquisite sensibility that the couple possesses.

There are beautiful objects all around me, gifts from the Natoris over the years, like the malachite glass vase now on Christopher's Steinway.

OPPOSITE Josie Natori is a woman of unparalleled humanity. For me, her eyes say it all. She is a very rare and special being. OVERLEAF The 17th-century Jacob de Wit *grisalle* is the focal point of one side of the spacious living room.

I believe that Fran and Art Reiner might be very surprised to learn that they played a significant role in my son Christopher's adoption. The family spirit at Macy's in the early years of my being there was totally captivating and even inspiring for so many of us. The people we worked with, the people we traveled on business with, the people who opened their homes to the rest of us were exactly what made that very special reality of belonging to something much more than a corporation so very unique and appreciated. The Reiners played no small part during this amazing period. They shared their family so graciously with me. The Reiners and I traveled to Santa Fe at one point and had the most wonderful time discovering the art of New Mexico. We traveled to the South of France and I have an amazing pair of brass palm trees, which once belonged to the socialite Mona Bismarck, from that journey. We traveled to places all over the world just as Cici Kempner had predicted for me years before—places I would have only been able to read about had it not been for Macy's.

I was lucky to spend a great deal of time with the Reiners at their New Jersey home with their extended family, including their two daughters, Melissa and Debbie. Fran might very well be the perfect mother, wife, and hostess and without any doubt, one of the best cooks on the planet. Whenever we were invited for a meal at the Reiner household, it was guaranteed to be a feast. Coming from a typical Italian family, I thought I had seen it all, but Fran always managed to take it to new heights. Besides surpassing anyone's expectations as a most accomplished cook, Fran decided she wanted to master the art of Chinese food preparation. Loving Chinese food, being a frequent guest at their dinner table was a dream come true. What got her interested in pottery I have no idea but I very much remember when she started taking lessons, studying with some of the most respected potters in the New York area. I have a number of her works in my home that I enjoy on a daily basis. Fran's modesty, to the benefit of her friends, kept her works out of galleries. But I truly believe some belong on permanent exhibition, they are just that fine. On one Christmas, the Reiners presented me with the most divine French brass champagne bucket. Every detail of it was perfect. I use it constantly, mainly because I adore holding it while looking at its two exquisite rams heads.

OPPOSITE The antique French ice bucket was a Christmas gift from Fran and Art Reiner many champagne bottles ago.

Art and Fran Reiner presented me with the most divine French brass champagne bucket. Every detail of it was perfection.

OPPOSITE Fran and Art Reiner were photographed at the black-tie 90th birthday celebration for the famous fashion designer Mollie Parnis that took place in Macy's executive suite. OVERLEAF The 19th-century seascape by an English artist that now hangs over the columned mantelpiece in the living room was the first gift I received for my first house from Cici Kempner. She said it reminded her of her home on the Galveston coastline, in Texas.

108

I have heard the phrase "It is not what you know, but more important, who you know" countless times. For me, getting to know His Royal Highness The Prince of Wales is the best evidence of the accuracy of such a statement. Joan Rivers had been a friend of the prince for a number of years before she and I became very close. As I remember, she was one of only two Americans who received an invitation to HRH's second wedding. As luck would have it, Joan and I enjoyed a friendship with Robert Higdon, the Director of The Prince's Trust, at the time. As the American director for the trust, Robert was based in Washington, D.C. The Prince's Trust is a foundation that he created to donate tens of millions of dollars to worthy causes. Once I became familiar with the trust, I was amazed by how few people were even aware of it and the good the prince had spread across the world through his charity. Many do not know that he possesses a sincere concern for the environment and the poor. Before the recognition of global warming became almost fashionable, the prince was already on the case out of a very sincere concern for our planet.

To assist in helping fund the trust, he created a business called Duchy Original. It was a natural and organic food product line very much in keeping with his concerns for our planet and its population. But I discovered it was rather poorly managed at the time. And the prince would be the first to tell me that once we met. Although the Duchy brand did have a very impressive sales volume, there were poor profits for the foundation. As a result of Joan's and Robert's urging, it was suggested that the prince and I should meet to discuss the business. Those in charge of the daily activity for all things relating to the prince at St. James Palace contacted me directly and made all the travel and accommodation arrangements.

So I was scheduled for a meeting and tea with His Royal Highness on a Saturday afternoon at his country home at Highgrove. I arrived in London the Wednesday before and immediately went through every store that sold the Duchy products and also checked out the competition. In my mind, it was very important to assess where and how Duchy was traded. You can sit in all the corporate meeting rooms in the world, strategizing your business, and look at all the numbers and products you like, but until you are on the selling floor or viewing the brand at retail, holding the product in your hand, or observing the consumers passing by not noticing your product, you have no idea where the opportunities might be to manage and move your business forward.

I was to arrive at 4 pm at Highgrove that Saturday afternoon for our very first meeting. Thank God, the director of the United States of The Prince's Trust would be joining us. There would be just the three of us. I was instructed beforehand as to the proper protocol while being in the company of a royal person—including how to exchange greetings and address His Royal Highness. Of course, I was very nervous. The only other experience that I can say surpassed the feeling I had at that point was the day I went to pick up my four-day-old son, Christopher. Of course we arrived on time at the front door of Highgrove House. A houseman greeted us and ushered us into a sitting room. The interiors were not at all what I

OPPOSITE The sterling silver enameled box, a gift presented to me by HRH The Prince of Wales, features his three-feather coat of arms that dates back to Prince Edward in the 14th century. The German motto at the bottom is translated as, "I serve." After getting to know Prince Charles, it became an honor for me to serve him.

Wishing you a very Happy Christmas
and New Year

and with immense gratitude
for all your wonderful help –

Charles and Camilla

I was amazed how few people were even aware of how much good HRH The Prince of Wales has spread across the world through his charity. Many do not know that he possesses a sincere concern for the environment and for the world's poor.

had expected—unpretentious and not grand in any way, just lovely and inviting in the way only the English are so brilliant at accomplishing. We were told the prince would be with us in a few minutes. I had never met a royal before, except for Princess Grace of Monaco. Before I could take in all the details of the room, the houseman reappeared, and asked us to follow him into the garden to meet with the prince. When he opened the door, I saw the prince standing on the other side of a very small reflecting pool.

He extended his hand. Greetings and introductions took place and the prince ushered us over to three wicker chairs and two wicker side tea tables. The first thought that came to mind was, "How do I find those tables for Connecticut?" Next to where the prince was seated was a small table with a gray file on it that said, "Joseph Cicio." Very CIA-looking, I thought. As soon as we sat down, the prince picked up the folder, which obviously contained much of my career background, but to my surprise also had a good deal of the press I had received over the years and magazine sheets with just about every photograph of my homes that had been published. I guess like any head of state he needed to be prepared before any first-time meeting.

Prince Charles immediately complimented me on my country house. But the statement that put me over the top was when he said, "Joe, this is just wonderful. It is obvious to me your homes were not done by interior designers. Is that true? I very much feel I could live there." I thought I would just die. What an amazing compliment coming from the Prince of Wales. He went on to ask if many of the objects he was admiring in the photographs came from family.

"No," I said. All the things came from a lifetime of traveling and collecting as well as cherished friends who tended to be very generous.

The planned 45-minute session went on for an hour and a half. We talked about Duchy extensively. We were both very candid. That is the only way I know how to operate, and the prince seemed to operate in the same manner. I was very prepared for our business discussion after my three days in London. Tea was served from the most wonderful creamware teapot. I had never seen anything like it. It was obviously an antique. Absolutely beautiful, I remember thinking. Towards the end of our time together, I shared my teapot observation with the prince. He looked at me with his wonderful smile and was obviously delighted that I had noticed it. "Oh yes, Joe, I just love it as well. It was a gift from my grandmother," he said.

As the meeting inevitably came to an end and we stood to leave, the prince looked at me eye-to-eye and said "Now, Joe, tell me, would you really help us? Would you consult on Duchy and direct a feasibility study for us?" My reply was very simple. "Sir, after this special time with you, I would weed your garden." He laughed. We shook hands, and Robert and I departed. "This man must have the worst press agent imaginable. He is nothing like I expected," I said. "It was totally delightful to be in his company. He is very smart and articulate and has a wonderful sense of humor."

The minute I got back to New York, I went to work. I made pages and pages of notes. I knew we needed to consult with the best to make this happen as professionally as possible. Our team put the feasibility study together in about seven months. The prince was very pleased and grateful. We would talk often on the phone during the weekend, when he had a bit more time. I remember being so impressed that he needed to know that we were approaching this exactly as he saw it.

I could not believe I was getting calls from The Prince of Wales at my home—Just "Joe, is that you"? He would also send many long, handwritten letters. Unfortunately, they were very difficult to read since his handwriting was even worse than mine. His Washington office and Robert's staff would do the translations after I faxed them the letters.

During one of my visits back to England, I was invited to dinner at Highgrove. On that occasion, I was also informed I would be sitting next to the Duchess of Cornwall. It was very exciting for me. I found her to be delightful. And if that was not enough, on another visit, I was invited to a small dinner at Buckingham Palace that the prince was hosting for the foundation. I just wanted to scream "Buckingham Palace!!!!"

On another evening, when Joan happened to be performing in town, we were both invited to Birkhall House, another country home that the prince's grandmother had given him. I would look at the chairs and imagine who had actually sat in them. Which member of the royal family? Which head of state? Which prime minister? I wondered if Churchill had ever been in that chair over by the fireplace?

When completed, my team and I made the feasibility presentation on the agreed target date in Philadelphia since the prince would be in Pennsylvania for another British royal event. Early on in my career I valued the importance of impressive, creative, and professional business presentations—always start off with a visual wow if at all possible. Of course, I wanted this one to be the best of its kind, with nothing left to chance and every detail impeccably thought out. Each specially designed tote bag had The Prince of Wales' coat of arms featured on both sides. As everyone entered the meeting room, the bags were the main feature on each of the boardroom chairs.

Later on that evening, the prince confided to me that the duchess had seen the tote bag when he got back to their suite and wondered if it was at all possible to get one for her since he had no intention of parting with his. Of course, I had always planned to have extras. All through the development of the study, I made sure the prince knew who the key players were on our team that had so graciously given their expertise and time to contribute to the mission.

The prince gave each of us a beautifully presented sterling silver box mounted in a wooden box with the coat of arms of The Prince of Wales. How could I look at the box and not recall these special events? Tea at Highgrove served by The Prince of Wales. Dinner at Buckingham Palace having a conversation with Patty Hearst. Joan teasing me to check to see if Patty had a gun in her purse. It was very important to me that our efforts and results made Joan and Robert proud of their recommendation. Only then could I say to myself, "Mission Accomplished."

OPPOSITE Receiving numerous letters and holiday cards from HRH The Prince of Wales, some of which now sit on a table in the living room, as well as his telephone calls to my home, were just not in any dream I could have imagined.

Thank you so much for your most helpful update on the feasibility study. It is very nice to know what is going on! I shall be fascinated to learn in due course whether it is felt we could handle the competition, bearing in mind the huge growth in the organic market, indicated by that article you sent.

It will also be most in-

OPPOSITE Christopher Joseph Cicio, who loved the camera, was photographed at home when he was 10 years old.

My son Christopher is the answer to my lifelong dream of having my own family. I was raised in a typical Italian middle-class family, with cousins, aunts, and uncles coming out of the woodwork, and I loved it. Family was everything as we grew up. We were all very close and there seemed to be a party or get-together at every imaginable opportunity. A new car, a new apartment, the successful outcome of a recent operation, or perhaps coming home from summer camp, just about anything would do. I always found it great fun, with the many colorful characters, endless dramas, and constant abundance of food—a good three to four times more than required. Cousins were more like siblings. And much to my amazement, funerals seem to have stuck in my mind as one of the most entertaining and colorful family events of all. While grieving and weeping widows, mothers, wives, sisters, and girlfriends were gathered around the coffin upstairs, many times to the point of being forcibly held back from jumping in with the deceased, the men were usually downstairs playing poker and feasting on delicious homemade dishes. And yes, no matter what any man might have thought or said, it was obvious that the women were the real power behind the domestic throne. I loved every minute of being part of this theatrical production. The voices. The vocabulary. The body gestures. The wardrobes. *The Godfather* movies came very close, but it was even better in real life. How did they ever get their hair to look and stay like that?

As the years went on and my career seemed to be on a very positive path, I remember one day being at a typical retirement reception for one of the Macy's executives and thinking that this would possibly be me someday. Then it hit me. What would I have to show for my mark in life? Just things and a lot of hard work. Then I recalled standing at the hospital bedside of my dying father. He was 96 years old and had led an amazing life that I have always thought most worthy of a screenplay. But what did I have? A successful career, some great friends, a house full of beautiful things? At the end of the day, I decided that was just not enough. There was nothing truly meaningful for me yet in my life. So I started down the road to making a momentous decision. I had dinner one evening at the New York Athletic Club with Dr. Peter Rizzo, a dear friend. At the end of the meal, I looked at Peter and confessed what I had been thinking of for some time. I wanted to have my own family. It was obvious at that point that the likelihood of this happening through the conventional route was not in the cards. Yet I wanted my own child. I remember asking Peter if he thought I had lost my mind. Like any loving friend, he went on for a few minutes about how amazing he thought I would be as a parent and why.

Peter got back to me after a few days and said he had spoken to a few professional associates whose counsel he valued. He said the first step should be for me to go see a good psychiatrist. First, to establish that my motivation was appropriate. Second, to ascertain that I was capable of dealing with the massive responsibilities that come with having a child and of making such a lifelong commitment. Third, should anything go wrong at any point during the process, or after, that I would be able to establish in a court of law that I had taken all the responsible steps. Peter suggested a Dr. Christopher Rise who proved wonderful to work with, and at the end of almost a year of weekly visits and everything from an inkblot test to quizzing me about why I disliked plastic flowers, Dr. Rise looked at me one evening and, rather to my complete surprise and huge relief, said, "You know, Joe, I think you should proceed. I truly feel you'll make a great parent." Even after all that, I remember walking out of his office that evening and thinking that there was no way on God's earth that this was ever really going to happen. This was early in 1987, a very different world then and one in which single gay men did not adopt. It was almost unheard of. I had no partner in my life and virtually no family. But I did have the most amazing group of close friends that never left my side. Yet I was not even sure how to proceed, especially as I was not prepared to consider any action that was not totally legal and aboveboard. I knew it would be difficult, and always thought it should be. After many, many disappointments with all the well-known agencies and numerous lawyers, I went back to see Dr. Rise. I explained how down I had become since I was not getting any younger and it just seemed no agency would even consider me as a viable candidate to adopt. I finally did connect with a reputable out-of-state adoption agency, recommended to me through Dr. Rise's sister, who had just completed her own adoption. Finally, after a few years of interviews and background checks, and more lawyers, it happened. At about 10 am on September 9th, 1990, I got a call in my office that told me I was now the parent of a beautiful, very healthy, seven-pound baby boy born that morning at 7 am. WOW!

I remember standing next to my desk completely stunned. Oh, my God, a baby boy. This was even more of a surprise given that two different clairvoyants had told me I was going to be the father of a baby girl. So much for them. It made no difference to me at all whether my child was a boy or a girl. Before the actual birth, I had traveled to England to engage a nanny, as British nannies have a reputation for being the best, as I knew that I would still have to travel for work from time to time. I wanted to be absolutely sure that I had only the best staff caring for my child in my absence. I also knew that my cherished group of wonderful female friends was always close by and would be on call. Everyone important in our lives received a complete, detailed itinerary of my travels, with all contact information, so that I could be reached at any hour, day or night. I took no chances, and was also blessed with an amazing administrative assistant, Rosemarie Clifford, who was actually the first to know (after Dr. Rise and Dr. Rizzo) that I was embarking on such a life-altering journey.

I have always loved the name Christopher, so much so that years before when it became time to select my confirmation name, I immediately selected the name Christopher. So I decided to name my son Christopher Joseph Cicio. I am Joseph Christopher Cicio; together we are CJC and JCC. I remember joking once how that would make monogramming the family silver easier. Meanwhile, Christopher was born outside of New York State and I had to take a short flight to go and collect my new baby son. I was a total nervous wreck. I took our English nanny, Helen, with me just to be sure I did everything correctly. I vividly remember sitting on the plane as it was about to take off and feeling like I had just consumed a bottle of lye. It was a most unforgettable day and I will always hold in my heart the memory of the moment when Christopher was brought to me for the first time. I was waiting in a reception room for new parents when the nurse walked in with this small bundle of beauty, all wrapped up, and handed him to me with a feeding bottle. He was only four days old and weighed seven pounds. "Congratulations, Mr. Cicio, this is your son Christopher," said the nurse. Babies were not new to me since I had been brought up with many children around me and had often taken care of my nine-years-younger sister since my mother always worked. But this

It is difficult to single out one special gift from my son. He surely is the lasting gift in my life. But the day when Chris discovered the wonderful black wood-carved hand perhaps impressed me the most. It took a certain amount of confidence at a young age to choose such an object.

was now my baby. I remember thinking he was about the most beautiful living thing I had ever seen. I started to cry. I quickly tried to control myself so I could feed him the little bottle of formula they had given me. "This is our first moment as father and son," I remember thinking. I just could not believe I had actually come this far and felt so truly blessed. I also remember thinking, "I hope I never wake up from this dream. This just can't be true." But through the grace of God, it was.

As a baby and young child, Christopher was straight out of central casting. Perfect in every way possible. Beautiful (of course), and with the most fabulously thick head of hair and a great smile. He was always happy. One of my most cherished memories is of checking in on him endlessly each evening while he was asleep, just to make sure he was breathing. Recalling the sight of Christopher with his face—and those adorable lips—pressed up against his pillow still gives me the most magical feeling. I always called him Christopher, and tried to get him to use "CJ," but as he grew older he preferred Chris and of course that is where we ended up. I had the kind of career responsibilities that required too many black-tie events and business dinners. But every evening I would get home in time to have dinner with Chris and then run out to the scheduled event. As the years went by, Chris seemed to develop so many talents, and always had the most endearing personality. It became apparent that he was very smart in school, accomplished on the athletic field in every sport—even the sports he didn't much care for. He was also very gifted musically. He took up a number of instruments, starting with the piano. One of our dearest friends, the fashion designer Josie Natori, was an accomplished classical pianist, and made sure he had the right instructor and, of course, a Steinway Grand. I noticed early on that Chris possessed a degree of sophistication that I certainly did not have at such an early age. He had a refined taste palate and seemed to know instinctively whether something was prepared correctly, just by tasting it. He was as happy with a slice of pizza as he was with smoked salmon or caviar. He also had a great eye and knew exactly what would please me when he chose a gift for me. I particularly treasure the memory of the very unceremonial wrapping in which each gift was presented. As a child, he would find any piece of paper and, with the help of miles of sticky tape, create his very own gift wrapping. I loved it, as it showed his great self-confidence.

It became apparent as time went on that this sense of self-confidence was something that was to stay with him as he became a young man. He hated the cold weather. I often thought of moving to California because of that, but have always been petrified of earthquakes. Also, my business was very much based in New York. Chris finally moved to California a few years ago to be with friends, and the warm weather, of course. I so miss the joy of giving him a hug, the smell of his hair, and to be able to kiss his head.

It is difficult to single out one special gift from my son. He surely is the lasting gift in my life. But the day when Chris discovered the wonderful black, carved-wood hand perhaps impressed me the most. It took a certain amount of confidence at a young age to choose such an object. I also loved that it was a perfect indication of how well he knew me. It is truly one of my most cherished possessions, along with the greatest gift of all—when he calls me Dad.

OPPOSITE A carved-wood hand, from my son. It amazed me in that a teenager would have such sophisticated taste.

Is there a face or a voice more recognizable in the entertainment business than that of Carol Channing? I don't think so. This was brought home to me when I went on one occasion with Carol to a very well-known New York plastic surgeon, as something had gotten into her head that it was time to have some work done, and she was afraid of going to the consultation alone. Having been down this road once before with a friend who had the same inclination late in life, I kind of thought I knew what might be coming. Dr. George J. Beraka had performed a number of procedures on well-known celebrities. But even more important was that he had tens of thousands of successful surgeries on mortals to his credit. What soon became very clear to me, however, was that he was not doing any of this work for public recognition. For Dr. Beraka, it was a most serious responsibility and perhaps even an art. I had always thought that the key to being a great cosmetic surgeon would be their hands—steady and creative. Dr. Beraka taught me that it is their eyes that are the crucial determining factor. They need to be able to assess their patient visually and decide not only where to go with their instrument, but where not to go. "Sometimes," confided Dr. Beraka, "less is a good deal more." After a considerable amount of time spent studying her facial details—Dr. Beraka looked her straight in the eye. "Miss Channing," he said, "I think to alter your face in any way would be a mistake on your part at this point in your life. Your face is Carol Channing. It is your career. Why fool around with such a great asset?" Carol was then in her early eighties and Dr. Beraka was completely right: she was recognized and respected in the world of show business for that amazing voice and for her characterful face and smile, with all its experience and personality. Carol was thrilled with Dr. Beraka's honesty, and we went off to a fun and lovely lunch.

I have always been a Carol Channing fan and have seen her in just about everything, but *Hello, Dolly!* will always stand out. I am convinced that David Merrick had to have been thinking of Carol for the lead role in that show when he and Jerry Herman first thought of taking it to Broadway in 1964. It was totally written for her, with no role more perfect for an entertainment icon like Carol than that of Dolly Levi. I absolutely loved the show and must have seen every Broadway production of it, from Carol to Ethel Merman, Pearl Bailey, Mary Martin, Angela Lansbury, and back again to Carol. Those other great actresses were all hugely entertaining, but to my mind no one could ever top, or even come close, to Carol.

Around 1989, my friend Denise Hale, who was once married to the director, Vincent Minnelli, decided she wanted to marry Prentiss Hale in a religious ceremony in a Serbian Orthodox church. Prentiss, who was then in very ill health and confined to a wheelchair, could not have cared less. Denise found what was possibly the only Serbian Orthodox church on the entire West Coast, conveniently in her home city of San Francisco, and asked me to join her at a meeting with the church officials. Denise got her way, and left very pleased with the plans for the forthcoming ceremony. After much planning, the wedding day finally came and proved to be beyond one's wildest imagination. Poor Prentiss was made to wear a heavy gold crown, as he then would be pushed down the aisle in his wheelchair, looking like some kind of aged King Arthur on a bad day. After the church ceremony, an evening reception was held at Stars, at that time the best restaurant in San Francisco. The guest list had plenty of A-listers from Denise's Hollywood days, when she was married to Minnelli, and a B list of those of us who had helped make her dream day come true. My great luck that day was to be seated next to Carol.

ABOVE Comedienne Carole Channing was captured on a cold day in New York wearing the coat I had made for her. Late night TV host David Letterman asked her if it had been made out of bath mats from Bed, Bath & Beyond.

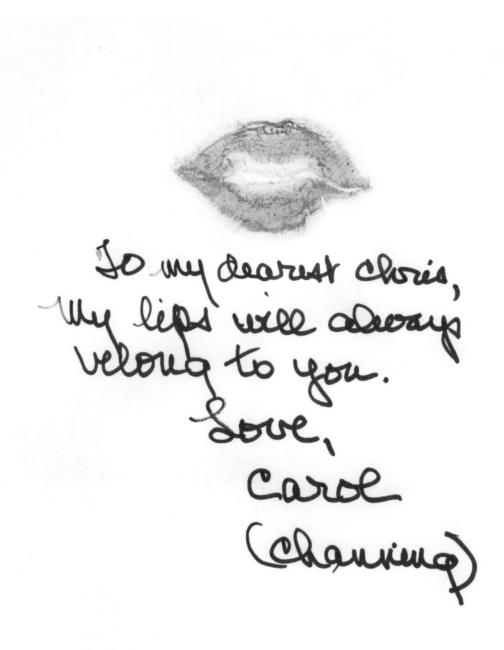

*To my dearest Chris,
My lips will always
belong to you.
Love,
Carol
(Channing)*

ABOVE Carole Channing's bright red lipstick kiss decorated an affectionate note she sent to my son, Christopher.

I soon realized that Carol was totally nuts, but nuts in the best way possible, my kind of nuts, and actually very intelligent and full of amazing stories. We hit it off so well that the other guests at the table started to get rather annoyed that Carol and I had so little time for anyone else around us. Carol had a particularly fabulous story about how Denise had fled from Serbia (then, Yugoslavia) by swimming out to sea. The most important and amusing part of the story was that Denise was busy swimming along with her grandmother's 20-karat emerald in her mouth. According to Carol, there was no way she was going to leave the country without it and Carol did the most hilarious impression of Denise speaking with her distinctive accent and an emerald in her mouth while swimming and trying not to swallow.

A long and lovely friendship started that day between us. At that time, Carol had been married for more than 30 years to her publicist husband–Charles Lowe. By all accounts, he was very successful financially, but no one, least of all Carol, had any idea where the money actually went. In 1998, after so many years of marriage, they suddenly split up. Carol was left with almost nothing except some very loyal friends and Chan, her only son (by her second husband, Alexander Carson). She owned five drawings by the celebrity caricaturist Al Hirschfeld. Despite several tries on her part to get the works back from a gallery on Madison Avenue in New York, she did not succeed. At a dinner at Al Hirschfeld's townhouse on Manhattan's Upper East Side, Al assured me that she was the genuine owner of the drawings. So I wrote an official-looking letter, which we got notarized, and which established me as Carol's legal representative, and took it with me to the gallery. Much to my surprise, I walked out of the gallery later that day with the five drawings. I had them sent to Carol in Los Angeles so that she could auction them off and pay a few bills. The late 1990s were difficult times for Carol. She had very little money and was not sure where to live. Around this time, Carol sublet a small apartment on Central Park South in Manhattan and tried to get her life back on track— never an easy task at the age of 77. My son Christopher and I would often take her out to dinner, to meetings, and to interviews dealing with her divorce proceedings, or to appearances on TV chat shows. Carol adored Christopher and was in awe of his natural gifts at the piano. She also taught him the joy of eating *moules marinières*. I have never really been into that kind of food myself, but can still see the two of them having a great time together in a bistro they both loved in the East Village. We also went to the theater a good deal. One year, winter fell upon us and dear Carol had no winter coat, so I had a wonderful white coat made for her out of the most outrageous fabric. It looked like a shag rug. She was scheduled to appear on *The Late Show with David Letterman* and I suggested she wear the coat out onto the stage. She loved the idea and I absolutely knew that she could carry the coat off with great aplomb, thanks to her height. When she came out on stage, Letterman took one look at her and asked, Why had she stopped off en route at Bed, Bath & Beyond for a little bath mat shopping? It was totally hilarious. The best part was that she was once again having a good time.

This house has lovely framed and inscribed photographs of Carol in almost every room. Most were gifts from Carol to Christopher and me and would arrive in those famous blue Tiffany boxes. My two favorites are one in the white shaggy coat and another, which, after inscribing the photograph, she kissed, leaving those glorious iconic red lips.

One of the most cherished gifts I received from my dear deceased friend, Peggy Tagliarino is the close relationships I share with her mother, Blanche, her sister, Betsy, and their extended family. As we know all too well, relationships such as these usually fade into the sunset of life's memories as time passes, once the unifying personality is out of the picture. In this instance, the links very much survived and, if anything, thrived over time. They are all just that special. Yet Betsy is the complete opposite of her sister Peggy. They looked nothing alike and had totally different ways of dealing with whatever life might throw their way. One loved shopping, the other did not. One loved food. The other could make you nuts over health concerns. One loved spending money. The other did not. And the list goes on. Besides having Blanche as their mom, the one important similarity between them was that they both possessed unlimited goodness and a very sincere, giving nature. They are by far some of the finest people I have had the joy of having in my life.

The truth is that Betsy missed her calling. There is no doubt in my mind that, had Betsy not succeeded in becoming a notable watercolor artist and teacher, she would have been very successful as a talk show host.

Much to my delight, Betsy is the kind of person who would often think nothing of taking the long drive from her New Jersey carriage house and art studio to visit her sister and their friends in Litchfield County, Connecticut. On each and every visit, Peggy would plan a friends and family dinner party or lunch—often perhaps both— that was guaranteed to generate over-the-top conversation on the all-important topics of the day, and of course, a wonderful feast. With Peggy, that usually meant a newly discovered recipe to experiment with every week.

Peggy's passing was devastating for all of us who were close to the family, for she was too young. Betsy had the daunting responsibility of organizing the sale of Peggy's home and its contents. On one visit, Betsy ushered me into the living room, the room that held more memories than any other. On the wall was my very favorite drawing, done by Peggy's former husband. Betsy asked me what I thought of it, and of course I answered honestly. This time it was very easy for me, with no need to be diplomatic. I have always adored it, was my quick response.

It truly looked like a Picasso. "Great," was Betsy's reply. "I thought you felt that way and I kind of remember Peggy telling me that you liked it a great deal, and that meant a lot to her, so I want you to have it as a remembrance of my sister. She would have wanted that." I was very overwhelmed and graciously accepted the drawing. This was not something I had expected. There are many things in my house that make me think of Peggy. And happily so. But this drawing always brings out the kindness of Betsy's heart—and not something I could ever take lightly.

PREVIOUS PAGES The talented artist Casey Childs drew the charcoal portrait of Christopher and me that anchors a wall in the sunroom. When I look at it, I see only Christopher. OPPOSITE When Peggy Tagliarino first showed me this drawing, I thought she had a small Picasso. Actually, it is a portrait of her by her former husband, Sam Tagliarino.

"I kind of remember Peggy telling me that you liked the drawing a great deal, so I want you to have it as a remembrance of my sister. She would have wanted that."

OPPOSITE Betsy Horowitz has a warm and infectious smile, and always-positive attitude. She is even more lovely in person.

I met Erté very early in my career. It was the fall of 1977, and a major party was being organized at the Metropolitan Club on New York's Fifth Avenue to celebrate the 85th birthday of this remarkable artist and designer. I was asked to design the party decor at the club and—most exciting of all—to coordinate a fashion show of costumes inspired by his art. The genius of Erté was no secret to me by then, but never in my wildest dreams had I ever imagined that I might experience such an amazing opportunity to meet him, and to become one of his friends.

The Metropolitan Club, with its dramatic center staircase, was the perfect stage for such an event. I instantly imagined a Ziegfeld production of cascading clouds of smoke rolling down those steps, with models featuring the Erté genius. That is exactly how it came off, with the added drama of Erté himself appearing at top center, humbly greeting the more than 500 notable guests from around the world. Of Russian descent, he was the tiniest person ever, impeccably groomed, and always wearing a brooch at the center of an embellished shirt neckline. As good fortune would have it, I was planning to travel to Paris on business soon after the party, and somehow Erté found out about my visit and invited me to his apartment for lunch. On the appointed day, I was nervous, with little idea of what to expect other than something rather grand and opulent. Much to my surprise, he lived in a very small apartment in an ordinary building in a Parisian suburb. From the outside, I was sure I had the wrong address. Yet this modest residence housed a lifetime of memories and a treasury of his art.

Because the apartment was so small, Erté had designed a series of moveable walls on which hung hundreds of his artworks. Through this creation, each of the works could be viewed with just the flick of a wrist. Almost as mesmerizing was his manservant, who was straight out of a 1920s silent movie, and had more than a hint of Erich von Stroheim. This lugubrious character served lunch, never seemed to take his eyes off his master or me and, of course, never said a word. It was all very theatrical—I loved every minute. After we had finished eating, Erté invited me into the main salon and presented me with a long cardboard tube, explaining that inside was an expression of his gratitude for all I had accomplished at the Metropolitan Club. Inside was an original painting of his celebrated *Alphabet Lady*, which he had created especially and dedicated to me. He later gave me a wonderful large signed self-portrait, which now hangs with his *Alphabet Lady* in my sunroom.

Erté was a humble and gentle man, very loving and generous to his close friends. Yet he knew what he wanted and how to get it. Following one of my suggestions, he collaborated with Martex, the linen and towel company, on a fabulous collection of beach towels based on his designs. The concept worked perfectly, everyone got along very well, and the towels were a great success. But I remember Erté calling me at my office one day wanting to see if I agreed with his negotiations. Martex had offered him a royalty on the number of units that were sold to the stores. His response was straightforward: "Gentlemen, I am 85 years old," he replied, "and care nothing about royalties. I care about cash!" His directness was rewarded with a handsome check. Thereafter, whether he visited New York or I went to Paris, we always got to spend time together, sharing lunches and dinners.

OPPOSITE A corner of the sunroom focuses on Erté's *The Lady in Red* (or *The Alphabet Lady*, as he called it). The original work was a thank you for the 85th birthday celebration I designed for him at the Metropolitan Club in New York.

What a truly great lady Peggy Tagliarino was. As I write this, I am looking at three photographs of Peggy taken within months of her passing several years ago. In each of the photographs, Peggy's smile is totally captivating. She was an unusual, positive force to all her close friends and family. She had that valued instinct to sense when something was not right with a family member or valued friend and had the divine intelligence and sensitivity to handle that awareness with total grace and true concern. We could always talk to Peggy, because not only was she very bright but also she was always there to listen. There was no hidden agenda with Peggy. All she wanted was to love her family and friends, and always be there for them. Her enthusiasm was intoxicating. Her loving mother Blanche would often say, "Peggy could get excited over a piece of string." When you were in Peggy's company, you just had to smile.

Peggy loved to entertain in her enchanting little Connecticut country house with dinner parties that were of a reasonable size so that all could participate in the conversation. She loved food and sharing her newest recipe discovery with those closest to her. Unsurprisingly, in her professional life, Peggy enjoyed notable success as a cookbook and restaurant publicist. She represented many of the greats known today, including Martha Stewart (who is known as not the easiest of clients). I would often tease her during one of her many entertaining planning sessions that she missed her calling and really should have been a cruise ship events coordinator, as she was always bringing people together. Unfortunately, Peggy did not have the best taste, as a glance into my gift closet would attest. Seriously, I thought, this woman has been to my home countless times. Does she really believe I am a guy who would welcome a purple plastic salad spinner? Or did I really need a horsehair whatnot box? In conversation one evening, planning her will, she asked me what I would want her to leave me. It was an easy decision. I simply answered, "Nothing." We both laughed and moved on. But one day she hit pay dirt. On that particular Christmas, she arrived with a wonderful bronze pod that I now love and keep in my sunroom on a stack of books. I never did find out who helped her pick it out. I am sure it had to be her friend, the designer Jeffrey Banks, during one of their many shopping sprees. But the most amazing gift she gave to her family and a few of her close friends was to bring us together for life.

Often, in tragic situations like this, after the link is gone, the human chain seems to go in different directions. Thanks to Peggy, we are as close as we ever were. Perhaps even closer. We are still Peggy's extended family, and every time we are together, Peggy is with us in her true spirit of love.

OPPOSITE Peggy Tagliarino gave me the bronze pod that is on a table in the sunroom—a perfect gift for her friend Joe.

On that particular Christmas, she arrived with a wonderful bronze pod that I now love and keep in my sunroom on a stack of books.
I never did find out who helped her pick it out.

OPPOSITE Truly one of the most intelligent friends one could possibly imagine, Peggy Tagliarino had the talent of careful listening down to an art form. Her smile was intoxicating and would immediately put everyone at ease.

For anyone interested in the history of fashion, women's liberation, keeping your head in a world of egotistical maniacs, the power of will and the creative spirit, the love of family and friends, generosity to others, a genuine enthusiasm for life, an appreciation of what youth can offer, of good food and a great sense of humor, then understanding the greatness of Eleanor Lambert Berkson is an absolute must.

I can't remember how and when I first met Eleanor. She had a wonderful apartment on Fifth Avenue and 87th Street, where she lived with little updating since the day she and her family had moved in. Here, she had entertained everyone from the Duke and Duchess of Windsor to just about anyone interested in learning about fashion or life in general. She knew I enjoyed real estate and I recall her telling me how she and her husband, Seymour Berkson, had purchased the apartment in 1944 for $14,000. After her death in 2003, it was sold for about $12 million. I so wish Eleanor had been here to experience the sale first hand. Eleanor raised her son Bill in that apartment and later on assumed responsibility also for her grandson, Moses, who wanted to come and live in New York. Can you imagine having Eleanor as your grandmother? It was a double-win situation. Eleanor had the youth she loved so much through the presence of Moses, and he got to know his grandmother in her inimitable glory.

At the time, I had the good fortune to live just two blocks away, on East 85th Street. "El" and I saw each other very often, and the most special times for me were always when it was just the two of us. Often we would eat at the small center island in her kitchen, which had not changed for over half a century. She still had an old wood-burning stove there. Mind you, there were also three refrigerators and a large freezer. El loved to cook and eat, and yet never seemed to gain a pound. The conversations were invariably fascinating and I marveled at how she always seemed to take such special interest in each of her friends and guests.

Sometimes we would just walk a few blocks away from her apartment to Jackson's Hole, an eatery we always enjoyed. She used to call me Dearie, which I loved and still miss hearing. "Let's go to Jackson's, Dearie," she used to say. El adored a good hamburger every now and then, and she had a particular soft spot for the rice pudding at Jackson's. It's worth bearing in mind that all this was going on at a time when El was well into her 80s and even well into her 90s. The hamburgers there were huge enough, but the rice pudding was beyond massive. It would come to the table in a large glass dessert dish complete with a saucer below to catch the overspill, and a mound of whipped cream on top to finish it off, cascading down the sides. Totally undaunted by the scale of what confronted her, El would tuck in with great gusto and finish everything off as though it were her last meal.

Knowing how much El loved food and cooking, I suggested one day that I drive her to the Fairway food market on West 125th Street for a shopping experience. She had never been there before and was excited to see it. The two of us walked into the market and each got a shopping cart. I can be a bit of a Jewish mother at times with my friends and was just a little worried, what with El being 95 at the time and toting a large Hermès Birkin crocodile bag that was always hanging open. I was slightly nervous for her safety and for the first few minutes

OPPOSITE This candid photograph of fashion public relations powerhouse Eleanor Lambert and me was taken when she was 88 years old. When she reached the age of 100, she was still sharing her plans for the future with me.

wouldn't take my eyes off her. Then she looked me intently and said, "Dearie, I will be absolutely fine. See you at the checkout." Needless to say, by the time I got to the checkout El was already there with a shopping cart piled high with goodies.

One of the most remarkable things about El was that she knew just about everyone, from all walks of life. She could regale you with stories about the time she stood in a town square in Germany and heard Hitler deliver one of his speeches. She could pick up the phone and get Queen Elizabeth II to take her call. Yet with all her greatness and all her contacts, she never gave any hint that these people were more important to her than the person she was enjoying being with at that precise moment. She was totally devoted to her close little family of friends. It could be Sunday evening with a group of six or eight of us watching the latest episode of *The Sopranos* in her little red TV room, or sitting in her dining room celebrating Chinese New Year with food just sent over by a relative of her friend Madame Chiang Kai-Shek, who owned a number of Chinese restaurants in New York.

When El celebrated her 99th birthday, on August 11, I wanted to do something special for her. There was, of course, a large "official" birthday celebration, with hundreds of people coming and going from her apartment throughout the day, but I wanted to organize a smaller and more intimate celebration, which I knew El would enjoy. I hit on the idea of taking her, Dawn Mello, and my son Christopher to dinner and then to a show at The Carlyle featuring Bobby Short, the cabaret singer and pianist. I called Bobby and told him what I was planning. Bobby made sure that our table was directly in front of his piano and he never took his eyes off El, seeming to sing and play every number to her. After the performance, he came and had dinner with us at our table. As exciting as that was for me, it was trumped by the lead drummer coming over to our table and handing my son Christopher his drumsticks while saying, "I was watching you, kid. You've got music in your blood. Enjoy these." Chris was only nine at the time, but he did have a great deal of musical talent and I guess it somehow showed that evening.

A year later, we celebrated Eleanor's centenary. A reception was held in her large Fifth Avenue apartment, once again with throngs of visitors dropping by all day long. It was truly a momentous occasion and rather like a national event, with calls, cards, flowers, packages, and telegrams arriving from all over the world.

Sadly, her health started to wane soon after that. She eventually needed the use of a wheelchair and spent a lot of time in bed. Yet her mind was as sharp as ever, something I was made very aware of one day. El had an almost childlike delight in opening gifts, so I would go up to her apartment about three evenings a week with a little something for her to open. I can see her now, with those bright blue eyes shining at me. On this particular occasion, I had brought her a pair of pink cashmere foot warmers. "Oh Dearie, they're just lovely," she exclaimed, and I could tell she meant it. I then came out with one of the more thoughtless comments I could have made, I guess. "El," I said, "I thought that when you're in the wheelchair they can keep your feet warm." Big mistake on my part. She immediately sat up straight in bed, looked at me fiercely, and in a very stern and forceful tone retorted, "You don't think I am

OPPOSITE I was one of two non-family members Eleanor Lambert mentioned in her will. The only thing I wanted was this drawing by Cecil Beaton, now on the mantelpiece in the sunroom, which I chose for sentimental reasons.

going to be in a wheelchair for the rest of my life, do you?" She was 100 years old. El died peacefully in her bed about three months later. I got a call from her son, the poet Bill Berkson, who told me, "Joe, you must know that Mama had you in her will," along with just one other non-family member. She wanted me to take whatever I wanted from her apartment as a token of her love and a remembrance of good times shared. I was so overcome by the gesture that I started to cry. I could not even put myself in the right frame of mind to think it through properly at that moment, so I asked Bill if I could get back to him in a week or so. Then that evening I was talking to a mutual friend and told him how humbled I was by El's expression of love. My friend advised me to make a decision as soon as possible. I suddenly remembered that when I used to sit with El in her bedroom, there was the most wonderful small pen-and-ink drawing by Cecil Beaton on the wall next to the headboard. It was one of the costume designs for Audrey Hepburn in *My Fair Lady*, my favorite movie and movie star of all time. Cecil and El had been great friends and he had given the drawing to her many years before. I nervously called Bill. When I asked him if he thought I could have the Beaton drawing, his reply was typical of the Berkson bloodline. "Joe," he said, "Mama loved you very much. The drawing is yours." I have cherished it ever since, not because of the divine Cecil Beaton but because each time I look at it I remember sitting at El's bedside, reading the hottest new story in *Vanity Fair*.

I got a call from her son Bill Berkson, who told me, "Joe, you must know that Mama had you in her will," along with just one other non-family member. She wanted me to take whatever I wanted from her apartment as a token of her love and a remembrance of good times shared.

OVERLEAF The dining room holds many memories, but my fondest one is the marble-topped sideboard that once held court in the English haberdashery company Turnbull & Asser department at the Bonwit Teller store in Manhattan. I could shop there only at sale time, of course. When the store closed permanently, I got the sideboard for $250. WOW!

Judy is the name everyone who knew Judy called her. She had to be not only one of the smartest, but also one of the sexiest women I have ever known. For a period of time, I had been working as an extra in the display department of Lord & Taylor. All that really meant is that I spent my time running errands all day long and sweeping up after the window designers. The most important errand was running across 38th Street to the Esquire coffee shop to get iced coffee, iced tea, hot coffee, and anything else you were told to bring back.

The fun errand for me was running down 38th Street to Hyman Hendler, the famous ribbon store. It was where every designer on Seventh Avenue or anyone in the fashion business would go to buy special ribbons and trim to adorn their creations. Even European designers would head for their door once they got off the plane. To be there was to step back in time. The four-foot eight-inches tall sales lady called Sadie liked me because she said I looked like her grandson. I was six-foot four-inches tall. We made a lovely couple. She was constantly giving me bags of amazing ribbons and trims. When I would go there to buy ribbons for the window fashion director, she would say "Here, Mamaleh, give this to your girlfriend." I would bring Sadie Lord & Taylor shopping bags and gift boxes. For Sadie, they were welcome treasures and my way of saying thank you. That was a big deal.

I guess the main reason I still have many of those beautiful treasures is because I never did have a girlfriend. Well, perhaps for a minute, but I was smart enough to keep the ribbons. To see the fashion director place the ribbons in a mannequin's hair or around the waist of a designer evening dress was awesome. If he thought a particular fashion silhouette needed a lift, he would add some trim to accomplish what he wanted for the window. Can you believe that designers would often come by to see their window and call in to find out where the trim came from? I had no awareness of the low rank I held in the department, I was just so happy to be working there. I thought that this kind of theater had to be the same as Broadway. To be able to be there and watch and learn from each and every designer doing their thing had to be better than being a student at FIT or Parsons. It was all happening before my very young eyes.

Each window designer had his own creative expression. They really were masters. I know you can learn a great deal in art or design school, but nothing could come close to the experience of being in the middle of it all in a store with such exceptional talent at that point in retailling history. Every time you turned around, you learned something new. Those were the days that windows on Fifth Avenue were a form of creative theatre. I guess I must have been good with a broom, since I lasted over a year as an extra, waiting for a full-time position to become available. I finally got my break and I was made mannequin boy—my first full-time job in retailing. I am sure the CEO of the store was just as pleased with his title as I was with mine.

All kinds of people were constantly coming and going in and out of the window department. Everyone was busy working with the deadline of the Thursday window changeover. One day, an absolutely stunning couple, a husband and wife team from Chicago, walked in.

OPPOSITE I believe Judy Neidermaier would very much approve of her table, set with the vintage English horns that were my first serious purchase for my first house. I found them in the now long-gone W & J Sloane store, across the street from Lord & Taylor. The horns cost me over three weeks' salary. Of course, that could never stop me.

ABOVE This photograph represents the true spirit of one of my all-time favorite lady friends, Judy Neidermaier.
She was one of the very first to support my career. Macy's would surely not have happened for me without her push.

Everything came to a halt and every head turned in their direction. Of course most heads turned toward Dale Neidermaier, who had a movie star quality—very tall, very tan, with blue eyes, blond hair, and a build like a football player.

The guys in the department would just die when Dale was around. Of course, I also thought he was gorgeous. But the one who really got my attention was his wife, Judy. She just seemed to have it all together—she was very attractive, with the most beautiful long hair that she worked beautifully, as she did with every other gift that God gave her—including a smile with wonderful Sophia Loren lips, and a body that would make any star jealous. She dressed perfectly, and you knew with one look at her that nothing was an accident. My good fortune in meeting her was, at the direction of my boss, to see what beverage I could get for her and her husband across the street.

But what won me over was her humanity and charm. I was a total nobody, running errands and keeping the place clean, but from Day One, she treated me as though I was the director. She was smart enough to understand that one never knows where someone might land in this business. As time moved on and my career advanced, we actually developed a lovely relationship. They were great company to be with, and as the years passed, we became very close. I would see them often when they would come to New York. At one point, Lord & Taylor started opening stores in downtown Chicago and the surrounding areas. It was always fun traveling to Chicago and being with Judy and Dale in their home base. They had two wonderful children and an absolutely beautiful home in Winnetka, Illinois. Whenever I was there, they would host a dinner party. They had a lovely antique dining table that I always liked, as it was not only beautifully scaled but also extended to seat up to 14 people. Judy knew I loved the table, and one evening she looked at me and said, "Joe, someday when we move I'm sending you this table." I never thought about it from that moment on.

Fast-forward about 25 years, and I get a call from my apartment building that there was a delivery for me from Chicago. To my total astonishment, it was the promised table. A number of years before, Judy had offered me a job with her company in Chicago. I had started to get very restless at Lord & Taylor, so I accepted her offer and was very excited about the idea of relocating. But days before I formally resigned, Judy called me, sounding very serious and business-like. "Listen to me," she said. "I just had lunch with a very interesting guy from Macy's. I gave him your name, among others, to call. They are looking for a new director for visual merchandising with big plans to make Macy's great again. You must know I would love to have you here in Chicago, but I love you enough to tell you I truly believe retailing is in your heart and soul, and wherever you are you deserve to be happy."

The man was Mike Stemen, who had just been brought over from California to be the director of stores at Macy's and who also turned out to be the best boss I ever had. Judy's table now sits in the center of my dining room and it is impossible not to think of Judy countless times every day.

OVERLEAF LEFT The house's original living room was turned into a paneled dining room. OVERLEAF RIGHT The 19th-century English sewing basket, with her personalized needlework on the inside cover, was a wedding gift from actress Mary Martin to Slim Keith and Leland Hayward. Slim Keith gave it to me on one of her weekend visits to my home.

Slim Keith and I talked every day and often two or three times a day. During one of our morning conversations, Slim's voice all of a sudden got kind of serious. "Now listen to me, darling," she said. "You are coming to dinner next Thursday evening." Slim knew that, as much as I adored her, I did not always enjoy the dinners at her penthouse at 32 East 64th Street. She also knew that I didn't like many of her so-called friends, who could be too self-involved, and that I would have little hesitation in declining. Most of them, I enjoyed much more on the big screen or on the stage but a good deal less in person. Yet I must admit that many were truly wonderful and entertaining. On these delightful evenings, it would be awesome to just be at her dinner table with such greats and feel so privileged to hear inside stories that would never find their way into print. Kenneth J. Lane, Mario Buatta, Brooke Duchin, Countess Romanones, Claudette Colbert, Bill Paley, Annette and Oscar de la Renta, Jerome Robbins, Gregory Peck, Mike Wallace, and, of course, Betty Bacall. Most of the time in their company, I would just sit there and occasionally pinch myself, for I knew this was a special and privileged experience and not to be taken lightly. The conversations were always very entertaining. Imagine sitting at the same dinner table with Bill Paley, the man who founded CBS, and listening to the good and the bad of Edward R. Murrow. Imagine Claudette Colbert whispering gossip in your ear about others at the table. Once I got over the thrill of sitting next to Claudette, I found her totally delightful. Then there often would be Sister Parish, the famous interior designer, smiling graciously and at the same time telling me, on the other side, who was unattractive and whom she disliked, which seemed to be just about everyone except Slim. She had no idea how truly funny she was. Whenever I was in her company, Sister Parish could remind me how easily she could have been an understudy for Margaret Rutherford in an Agatha Christie movie.

I have always considered it bad manners to reply to a dinner invitation with "Who else is coming?" and Slim knew my point of view in such matters, so I would try desperately to navigate the conversation and learn more without being obvious. But I was never any match for the very clever Slim, who didn't give me a chance to say, "Thanks, but NO thanks" and quickly added, "I want you to meet Gene Hovis." The name was not familiar to me. And Slim went on as to why I needed to meet Gene. "He is a brilliant food authority and an amazing chef," adding, "you need him at Macy's." So there it was. Gene needed Macy's more than Macy's needed Gene, it seemed in Slim's eyes. Of course, there was no way for me to decline. During cocktails on this special evening, Slim took me by the hand and brought me into her kitchen to meet her old friend, Mr. Hovis. There he was, cooking his heart out—a tall, black, and very attractive gentleman with the best smile ever. Even with an apron on, he looked impeccable. I wondered how he could look so great and work so hard in this very small New York kitchen. I later learned that Gene's specialties in the kitchen were many of my favorite dishes. He was from the South and well trained in the art of food preparation by a beloved aunt. He served Virginia ham, macaroni and cheese, ribs, cornbread, and all the trimmings. God knows I had had all these things many times before, but after that evening I can say in all honesty I do not remember anything I enjoyed more than the dishes prepared by Gene-

OPPOSITE Food authority and chef Gene Hovis was photographed standing between Eleanor Lambert, on his right, and Brooke Hayward Duchin at a glamorous black-tie event hosted by Count Volpe in Venice, Italy, in 1993.

Hovis for Slim's guests and at, as it turned out, his first Macy's audition. He ended the meal with his famous Gene Hovis lemon cake. There was just nothing better. Everyone ate too much and we all went home completely satisfied. Wasting no time, Slim called my office the next morning about 10 am. "So, my darling, what did you think of Gene and his food?" No hello from Slim; she was on a mission. Of course I told her how wonderful I felt everything was and of course how impressive Gene seemed on many levels. Not only was he very capable in the kitchen but also he was extremely personable. "Good," she said. "Can you get him a job at Macy's in the food department"? I quickly asked her to just step back some and give me a little time to think this through and consider if there were any viable opportunities. I called Slim a day or two later and said I think I have it. I explained that I had no authority at Macy's as far as hiring anyone within the food division. As a result, strategy would be paramount. There was no question Gene was an amazing talent. There was also no question in my mind that at that point Macy's actually needed serious help in their food areas. So Slim's timing was perfect, as things turned out. Slim was too smart and knew me all too well not to have anticipated how I might react. I soon became aware that, besides knowing his craft well, Gene seemed to know anybody who was anybody. But I also knew his and Slims' social circle would not normally think of Macy's as a shopping alternative. So in my mind, it was a win-win situation for Macy's and Gene if I could possibly make the alliance happen. So I went on to present my strategic plan to Slim. Edward Finkelstein, the CEO of Macy's, enjoyed a good meal perhaps better then breathing. But to make something this complex, and at that level of executive placement happen, one needed to make Ed think it was his idea. "Let's plan a dinner party in my apartment and ask Gene to be a guest but he also must prepare the food," I said. The guest list would be Finkelstein's executive team for balance. We would also get Betty Bacall to be there and place her to Ed's right, and Brooke Duchin or Slim to his left. That level of glamour and celebrity would be very helpful in putting Ed in the most receptive frame of mind. We invited a few more from our "A" list, like Kenny J. Lane, who was always great fun to dine with. We had to have Bobby Short, who was a good friend of many on our list and adored Gene. Since Bobby was performing nightly at the Carlyle Hotel, he could not be there for dinner. But I begged him to come for coffee and dessert, as my apartment was only a few blocks away from the Carlyle. All our celebrity guests were made aware of our little Gene Hovis/Macy's plan and who the key players in this production were. Fortunately, at this point, Ed knew Slim reasonably well, both having enjoyed many dinners and lunches at my country home. Gene outdid himself that evening. The food was amazing and it seemed we laughed from start to finish.

I usually arrived at my office each morning between 7:30 and 8:00 am. Ed arrived every morning with his car and driver at 8:45 am. My office was a few doors to the right of Ed's on the executive floor. Almost holding my breath, I hoped Ed would summon me to relive the evening before. He did that sort of thing many times. Now it had to come from him. As though we were following a writer's script and the cameras had started to roll, it happened.

OPPOSITE A rare landscape by Edward Molyneux, who was not only an accomplished artist but had his own couture fashion house in Paris until his death in 1974, now hangs above the fireplace in a corner of the dining room.

I spotted this lovely French landscape painting while enjoying my coffee and went over to check out the price. It was a bit over my budget. But that was not something that usually slowed me down.

Ed's secretary Veronica called me at 8:40 am and asked me to meet Mr. Finkelstein in his office since he had just called her from the car and it would be minutes before he would be coming up in the elevator. I went down to his office just as he walked in. We exchanged good morning greetings and I just stood there. He sat back in his big leather chair and proceeded to tell me what a wonderful dinner party last evening was and how amazing he thought the food was. I just could not believe what he followed with next, and so quickly. "Do you think we could use Gene in the Macy's organization? If so, where?" he asked. Ed had a natural inclination to think out of the box. I tried to look somewhat surprised and yet thoughtful. "Ed, I think that is brilliant. God, I wish I had thought of it." I remember thinking that, since I was standing next to a pair of exterior glass French doors, lightning was about to come through those doors and God will get me for this. But God must know I am doing this for Macy's, Slim, and Gene, right? I thought. Then Ed and I proceeded to discuss strategy as to how to make this happen. Soon after some hilarious private tutoring classes by me with Gene on how to respond in a corporate interview, the rest was history.

Gene joined the organization and quickly started to make storewide contributions that were newsworthy. I had an office space created for him directly behind our famous Corner Shop, with his own small kitchen. I created a celebrity room in the antiques department that could be closed off with French doors. There, we could host Gene Hovis celebrity lunches while customers could peer through in awe. Imagine seeing Gene serving his famous chicken pot pie and lemon cake to the likes of Jessye Norman, Bill Blass, Mario Buatta, Lauren Bacall, or André Leon Talley! Soon, Gene was a true Macy's family member. Since Gene's amazing lemon cake was doing so well, I decided that we should take this lemon cake on the road to many of our branch stores. The Macy's food merchants were able to get me in front of Dromedary Food with my goal of mass-producing the cake so we could sell it by the thousands in all stores. Our graphics and packaging division got to work and designed the most perfect packaging for the cake, with Gene's picture on the box, bow tie and all.

Years later, after I had moved to I. Magnin, Gene decided to retire to his home in Hudson, New York, with his partner, Hans Teets. They opened a small antiques store on the main street among all the other trendy shops. I remember well the day I was sitting in front of Gene at a desk in the front of the shop. Gene was a snob, without a doubt. A handsome, lovable, funny and talented snob, and he was well aware of it all. I spotted this lovely French landscape painting while enjoying my coffee and went over to check out the price. It was a bit over my budget. But that was not something that usually slowed me down. After a few hours of negotiation, I took it home. Of course I knew there was no way I was walking out of his establishment without a purchase. After all, that is what friends do for friends. I have enjoyed that beautiful painting ever since my visit with Gene in Hudson. Sadly, Gene passed some years ago. But the painting now in my dining room never fails to bring his smiling face and the fun of being with him back to me, with great joy.

Blanche Levine might be about the chicest woman I have ever met. Even at 95 years of age, I defy you to guess that she is a woman beyond her sixties. Now living in Palm Beach, Florida, in an absolutely exquisite home surrounded by memories of a lifetime of joys, survival, and privilege, she is not without the memories of the loved ones she cherishes to this day. She has never let a day go by, she told me, without a smile recollecting the special relationships that she holds in her heart. I first met Blanche through her eldest daughter, Peggy Tagliarino.

Much to my good fortune, Blanche would often come to visit Peggy at her country home in the hills of Litchfield County before Peggy's tragic and unexpected passing a few years ago. Always planned around every Mother's (as Peggy would always refer to Blanche) visit would be every lunch, dinner, and daily outings to nearby points of interest.

Besides being well-read and highly intelligent, Blanche was also very quick-witted. In the early years of my getting to know Blanche, I would notice that she would often just seem to disappear from our little group discussions at Peggy's home. At first, I would be slightly concerned until I searched her out one afternoon only to find her outside standing in front of the garage, smoking her heart out. I was truly shocked. I recognize how difficult addictions can be, but smoking somehow usually puts me over the top and I would always say so. I have seen more than my share of pain and suffering in those who could not shake this addiction. "Blanche," I said, "I can't believe with all you have going for you that you are actually smoking. Don't you know that it will kill you?" "Darling," she said with her lovely smile. "Don't you know I am in my late eighties, in perfect health, and standing in front of you, which must at this stage of my life prove something? Obviously God is just not ready to deal with me yet. Or more likely, can't decide where to put me."

Immediately after Peggy's passing Blanche could not enter Peggy's house again. It was too much for her and understandable to all who loved them both. I went only once myself, at Betsy's request, and I promised myself, never again. Somehow it is one of the worst experiences to endure. Too many memories of joyous times that you know can never be again. So when Blanche needed to come back to our area of Connecticut, I was delighted to offer her what I have always called the Slim Keith Guest Suite in my home. Very much fitting accommodations that I felt Blanche truly deserved. On one such visit early on, Blanche arrived with a gift box for me to open. In it were five amazing black intaglios framed in brass. Obviously, she had been in my home many times and knew of my intaglio collecting passion. Despite being a collector and having traveled much of Europe searching out intaglios, I have never seen intaglios such as the beauties Blanche arrived with that day. They are unique in every way possible, from fabrication to presentation. Of course I am delighted to have them and be able to add them to my collection. But when I look at them, what I very much focus on is knowing the grief Blanche held in her heart for her daughter Peggy, and with that grief yet had the presence of mind to think of me in such a generous and gracious way. They are only very special because Blanche Levine is very special, indeed.

OPPOSITE During her first visit to my home, Blanche Levine toured each of the rooms carefully. When it came to my large collection of intaglios, she stopped and asked many questions about their history and fabrication. Little did I know what she had in mind—until on her next visit, she appeared with these rare 19th-century black intaglios.

I have never seen intaglios such as the beauties Blanche arrived with that day. They are unique in every way possible, from fabrication to presentation.

OPPOSITE Blanche Levine was photographed at home in Palm Beach, Florida. She checked the stock market daily.

ABOVE Betty Bacall always enjoyed our annual Christmas carol sing-a-long at the Duchins' loft in New York. The cast each year was not to be believed—imagine singing next to violinist Isaac Stern or opera singer Renée Fleming.

Of course, I was introduced to Lauren Bacall—known as Betty to her close friends—through Slim Keith. I say, "of course," because the two women were the dearest of friends. The first time I met Betty was at Slim's bedside in the intensive care unit at New York Hospital. Because Slim did little to prolong her own life and was absolutely addicted to smoking cigarettes, she was often in the hospital. And if Slim was there, so was I. No matter what the medical prognosis, Slim always appeared to be in good spirits, but truth be told, she would often get very down and feel sad and depressed. Betty seemed to be one of the very few friends, out of a cast of thousands, who could bring Slim out of her melancholia and make her laugh.

Once I got to know Betty well, I realized that she and Slim went so far back that they often seemed to be sisters. After all, it was Slim who was credited with having discovered Betty on the cover of *Harper's Bazaar* and pointed her out to her husband at the time, the famous film director, Howard Hawks. She passed him the magazine and said, "I think this is worth looking into. This girl has it." Little did Slim realize that she and Betty were so similar in terms of style, humor, intelligence, and beauty, and in the early days, they certainly looked alike: two absolutely stunning beauties. Both were very quick-witted and shared an identical sense of humor, often rather edgy and sharp.

As a result of Slim's comments, Howard was to cast Betty opposite Humphrey Bogart in his 1944 movie *To Have and Have Not.* Throughout the film, Bogart addresses Betty as Slim, and the story gets even better, as told to me years later by Slim and Betty. Apparently, one afternoon, Howard came home for lunch after filming at the Hollywood studios and found Slim in the bedroom, reading. "Where's the two-piece suit you just purchased?" he asked, "the one with the small black-and-white checks?" Slim replied, "Over in that closet, why?" "Well, I want to try it on that kid you told me to screen test," he replied. So it came to be that Betty was to wear Slim's suit in the film.

During the making of the film, "Bogie" and Betty began a romance that was to culminate in their marriage the following year. He was the great love of her life, and she was terribly depressed following his death in 1957. She told me once about a trip she and Slim had made to Acapulco, Slim having suggested that the two of them go away for a few days to a far-flung place where Betty could escape the press. Little did Slim know that leaving her husband, Leland Hayward, in the dubious care of Pamela Harriman during her time away with Betty was going to have grave consequences. Pamela had her own plans, and while Slim and Betty were in Mexico having a great time, Pamela and Leland were enjoying themselves in New York. Slim's marriage to Leland was to end soon after.

Meanwhile, down in Acapulco, Slim and Betty were having a lovely meal in the hotel dining room, with plenty of champagne, good food, and lively music. On seeing these two beauties dining alone, a very handsome Latin type approached their table in the hope of joining them for a drink. He did, and it soon became obvious that he was more interested in Betty than in Slim. Never believing three to be company, Slim excused herself and went back to the two-bedroom suite she was sharing with Betty, so that she could get into bed and do some reading. Some time later, the gentleman—if one could call him that–escorted Betty up to her suite for what she was hoping would be no more than a simple goodnight kiss. But, our Latin friend had much more in mind. He forced himself into the suite and then proceeded to chase

Betty around the living room for rather more than just a kiss. Slim always kept her bedroom door open a little in order to be sure Betty got back safely, and as Betty was busy navigating herself away from her would-be Latin lover, she was repeatedly passing Slim's door and screaming out for help. Slim was laughing her head off. She knew that Betty could take care of herself. Or could she? On about her fourth lap around the room, Betty shouted out to Slim, "Help me! How the hell do I get rid of this guy?" Slim's reply was simple. "There's only one way, my dear," she purred. "Let him catch you." That response sums up Slim and Betty. They were friends to the end, and, along with Brooke Hayward, Betty and I spoke at Slim's memorial service in 1990, held at the Burden Mansion on New York's Upper East Side.

Anyone who knew Slim would tell you that she passed away much too early, but my friendship with Betty somehow helped continue my relationship with my lost friend. Betty and I enjoyed many quiet dinners with Gene Hovis and Brooke Hayward, and Gene and I also escorted the ladies to a number of black-tie functions. The most memorable was the opera season-opening gala held at Lincoln Center in 1991. I had never been on a red carpet before, and to have Lauren Bacall on my arm, with untold numbers of photographers firing off their camera flashes in front of us, was a pure movie moment for me.

My most cherished memories of Betty were when Gene and I would put together an early morning basket of homemade donuts (Betty loved them) and Thermos flasks of good coffee, and venture over to The Dakota on West 72nd Street, where Betty had an apartment. We would sit in her kitchen with our homemade breakfast and do almost nothing but laugh and tell stories. I had never been in a Dakota apartment before visiting Betty. I remember the first time she opened the door and greeted us, without make-up and wearing an old robe, with her grey hair pulled back. After we left, I said to Gene that Betty could haunt a house looking like that. But, in fact, I felt honored that she felt so comfortable with us that no frills were necessary. The apartment was amazing, and one of the few left that had not been subdivided. It was so enormous and rambling that I suggested to Betty that she keep a box of breadcrumbs at the front door so that one could find the exit. She was clearly a collector—pewter in one hallway, faience in another, Delft somewhere else. It seemed to go on and on, and I don't think I have ever seen so much gathered together in one home. The room that really blew me away was the dining room. Not only was it huge and overlooking Central Park, but it was filled with dozens of sculptures by Henry Moore. There were also lots of Moore drawings.

I have some lovely things given to me by Betty, but I think my favorite is a rather unusual mirror that she received from her mother for her first apartment. I love how that mirror brings Betty back to me. I can still hear her distinctive voice. She was the last of her kind. She enjoyed a career full of accomplishments, but also with some regrets—yet I do not think that you can ever really appreciate life if you have not experienced disappointment. There is no doubt that the real joys in Betty's life were her family and Humphrey Bogart, and whilst there are a number of doubtlessly very talented actresses today, I struggle to find many—or any— with her class, abundant qualities, and interests in so many things.

OPPOSITE The delicately-executed mid-19th-century rare sterling silver lace cigarette box was a gift to Lauren Bacall from one of her admirers at the height of her career. One morning, when I visited her at her home in the famed Dakota apartment building in New York, she generously offered to add it to my select collection of silver objects.

I have some lovely things given to me by Betty, but I think my favorite is a rather unusual mirror that she received from her mother for her first apartment. I love how that mirror brings Betty back to me. I can still hear her distinctive voice.

OPPOSITE Lauren Bacall was very young when she moved from her mother's home in The Bronx, to her first apartment in Manhattan. Her mother was very concerned that she have a good mirror to do her make-up, so she went and got her one. A lifetime later, as we rummaged through some of her closets in the Dakota, the mirror appeared. Betty said, "What do you think of this?" I replied that I liked it because it was different. "Good," she said, "so are you, so take it."

As you might expect, the main floor of Macy's Herald Square store is very large—a total of 105,000 square feet, running from Broadway to Seventh Avenue and from 34th to 35th Streets. The volume implications of a business the size of Macy's main floor at the time placed a great deal of pressure on the shoulders of the merchants responsible for any assigned selling space on that floor. Added to that, they had new management who were determined to change the Macy's image to that of a more upscale retailer. Many in the marketplace felt that a moon landing was more achievable than with the Macy's of 1976.

I remember my second day there, and the exact spot where I was first introduced to Rosemarie Bravo, Macy's fragrance buyer at the time. She had about the best smile I had ever seen and possessed that aura of enthusiasm that most great merchants have. It did not take me long to understand that I was in the company of not only a very competent merchant, but also an individual who enjoyed the people and family around her as much as her career.

I am very good with retail spaces and have a better-than-average ability for identifying opportunities for what is known as "four-wall productivity": How to use all of the merchandising space to the best possible commercial advantage. Rosemarie figured this out even before I did, and would constantly get me down on her selling floor for walk-throughs. We would march up and down each aisle, assessing the space and merchandising counter configurations in the hope of developing increasing sales opportunities. In cosmetics and fragrance, every inch has volume implications.

Rosemarie would get me to meet her at early-morning vendor meetings, often at 7:00 or 7:30 am, with the intention of getting that new fragrance launched before the competition got the chance. Being the first to launch a fragrance or treatment line in your store gave you the competitive edge. She loved blueberry muffins and I loved eating, so I would try to get into work before she did and surprise her with a freshly made muffin on her desk. At the time, I had a wonderful administrative assistant, Laura Manachetti. Laura was also a member of the early-arrival club and had developed a great relationship with Rosemarie, often leaving with her in the evening long after I did, hardly ever before 8:00 pm, an early departure by Rosemarie's standards. It did not take Rosemarie and me long to become close friends—very easy and natural, perhaps due to the fact that we both came from typical Sicilian families. I quickly grew to feel toward her parents, Ann and Ben, as close as I could to any blood relative.

It was Rosemarie who first got me interested in fragrance bottles. I had started a fascination with fragrance back in my Lord & Taylor days when, for some reason, we would test ourselves (and then our associates) on being able to identify a brand just by the fragrance. I just loved getting in an elevator and being able to identify what fragrance a fellow passenger was wearing. Whether male or female, it was always great fun. Macy's elevated my exposure to that world. Rosemarie's first fragrance gift to me was the amazing *L'Air Du Temps* from Nina Ricci in that iconic Lalique double-dove bottle. There is no question that it is the jewel in the crown of all bottle collecting. I have no idea how many others she gave me after that. She knew I had started collecting bottles and made sure I got the newest introduction every time.

OPPOSITE I don't believe there has ever been a fragrance buyer more capable than Rosemarie Bravo. This in-depth collection of designer perfume bottles would have never come to be were it not for her love and generosity.

Over the years, as both Rosemarie and my careers moved on, I was given many bottles for different reasons. These ranged from typical goodie-bag gifts at industry events, to signed, limited-edition bottles from fashion designers who had created their own fragrances. The bottle from when I had lunch with Sophia Loren, when we introduced the Italian movie star's fragrance at Macy's, is surely at the top of that particular list. Or perhaps the time we introduced Thierry Mugler's *Angel* fragrance at I. Magnin, and I was amazed that it sold to almost as many men as women—very smart—a great fragrance with no gender.

It is great fun for me to gaze upon my collection of bottles. Rosemarie comes to mind immediately. What always follows is the joy of recalling the many Christmas Eves my son Christopher and I spent at her home with her husband Bill Jackey and their family. It was a real family spirit that I cherished and valued very much for my son. Chris absolutely loved being at their home. Early on, Bill would get dressed up as Santa Claus and try to surprise Chris, but he was not a match for Chris. "You're not Santa—you're Bill" was his quick assessment.

In the mid-1980s, Rosemarie's career gained great momentum and she was promoted to various additional responsibilities within Macy's. I remember watching her career advance and thinking that there was no question she would end up someday as the CEO of a major business. And the day Macy's purchased I. Magnin, the California specialty store, Rosemarie was appointed CEO of the new acquisition in San Francisco. Later, she became the President of Saks Fifth Avenue, where she managed to build a formidable organization and bring profits to a new high. Later still, she agreed to take on the responsibility of being the CEO at Burberry in London. Burberry was a very old and very tired brand that had lost its way over the years and was losing money hand over fist. But Rosemarie could see its potential and, as with everything else she had taken on before, she totally dedicated herself to the task. She moved to London with the ever-present support of her husband Bill, built a new dynamic team at Burberry, traveled the world, and rebuilt one of the top fashion brands in the designer market.

OPPOSITE I was photographed next to Rosemarie Bravo, the newly appointed CEO of I. Magnin, and Tye and Rosita Missoni, the famous Italian knitwear designers, when we toured the specialty store in San Francisco, in 1992.

Bill Blass was already a major fashion celebrity when I first met him. I believe it was 1964, and I was a very young extra with Lord & Taylor's window display department. The store was coordinating a Bill Blass fashion show luncheon in the grand ballroom of the Pierre Hotel on Fifth Avenue, and my assignment was to help backstage by ensuring the models went out onto the runway with all the correct accessories. Being backstage was much more exciting than being out front, because the designer was always there doing last-minute adjustments before each model was sent out. Bill had a natural ability to make everyone working backstage feel at ease. He was always a true gentleman, grateful for our help, and he showed it.

I remember thinking back then that Mr. Blass was the most dashing gentleman I had ever seen, other than in the movies. He always had a cigarette hanging out of the side of his mouth, which at the time was the height of style and glamour, with no one talking about how smoking was detrimental to one's health. And in Bill's case, it would prove to be fatal.

The first time Bill properly noticed me was, I think, when I had just started at Macy's in the spring of 1976. Macy's was hosting a cocktail party on the CEO's executive floor to mark the introduction of a line of Bill Blass bed linens. That sounds like nothing today, but for Macy's back then it was truly a very big deal, as important designer labels always went to Bloomingdale's, and with good reason. Macy's had problems that ran from serious union restrictions to unbelievable consumer demographics. Few discerning shoppers ventured down from the Upper East Side to 34th Street for anything, let alone to visit Macy's. That was the reason I was lured away from Lord & Taylor to be the creative force as the newest member of a very dynamic team of merchants and operations specialists, led by the relatively new Macy's CEO Edward S. Finkelstein.

I had been on the job for just a few weeks when I was told about the Bill Blass cocktail party being planned on the executive floor of the 34th Street store. I knew that Bill's collection required an awesome presentation. Instead of following the public relations department's suggestion of showing samples of the bedding on easels, I decided—as the party was to be attended by many retail industry leaders and the trade press—that I had to address two major objectives. First, we needed to start generating headlines in the trade papers that there was a new retail team at Macy's with creative support that intended to give the uptown store and their customers a run for their money. Second, I wanted to create a storewide buzz by telling the Macy's organization, from the bottom up, that there was a new creative guy in town who had the ability to attract and direct a team that could, and would, generate newsworthy creative results for their big store and help enhance the business at the same time. So, no easels, I told my people. Instead, we would build four "Bill Blass rooms" on the executive floor, creating a total environment for each design and running from traditional to contemporary with each pattern. I called in many industry favors and at the same time spent the entire spring budget on that one event. It was nothing more than a throw of the dice for me, but it was too important not to take the risk. This was my first creative opening. If it did not work well, then

OPPOSITE Fashion designer Bill Blass found the 19th-century bird drawing, now in the powder room, at a French antiques show, and gave it to me on a snowy Christmas evening. OVERLEAF A reporter from *Home Furnishings Daily* stood between me and Bill Blass at the Macy's party that introduced the first Blass bedding collection for Spring.

I didn't belong there and living while skiing in Vermont full-time was not such a bad thing after all. As I look back, I can smile with complete delight and wonderment at just from where in hell did I get the inspiration to venture in that particular strategic direction? Everyone in the business started talking about the new goings-on at Macy's. Through a great deal of trade press coverage, and the resulting buzz, it was not hard to see that we were on our way, both in the marketplace and especially within the Macy's organization.

Bill Blass was very impressed by what he saw at his cocktail event at Macy's. There were four rooms, each very different, but all playing to the designer's creations and to the consumer who would be attracted to each specific line of bedding. That event marked the start of my friendship with Bill. He was not only impressed by what we had achieved but also very grateful. As the years progressed, much to our delight we found ourselves neighbors in Connecticut. Bill was truly a lovely man, always there for his friends, and invariably to be relied upon to offer a very wise and honest point of view for any question asked of him. He was very well-read and could hold an intelligent conversation on just about any subject. I used to love our one-on-one lunches in the Garment District of New York and the fun dinners we had, both at Mortimer's in New York, with Glenn Bernbaum, and often in Connecticut. Just imagine Jessye Norman singing at Bill's Christmas dinners in the country. It was always pinch-your-arm time for me.

I have a wonderful bird drawing from Bill, presented to me very unceremoniously during Christmas week 1995, when I was hosting a dinner at my home. I had planned an evening with a wonderful collection of Connecticut friends, 14 of them, if I remember correctly, all to be at a large round table, my favorite seating for a dinner party. Bill did not drive, so he always either had a driver or one of us to pick him up and take him home. When he arrived for dinner, and when I was greeting him at the door, I noticed a package under his arm that was protected with some kind of shipping paper. No twine, ribbon, or tape. "Here," he said, "I hope you like this because I do and want it back if you don't." No chance of that, I immediately thought. It was a very unusual color drawing of a bird. And it was a gift from Bill Blass.

There was a terrible snowstorm that evening, yet, much to my surprise and delight, everyone arrived. Unfortunately, Gene Hovis, who was coming from New York, and had planned to arrive at 2 pm (since he was cooking) arrived at 8 pm. Bill, a man who was not an evening person, could not wait any longer for Gene's glorious fried chicken. So he walked into the kitchen, found some foil, took four pieces of chicken, placed his not-so-little package in the side pocket of his exquisite Savile Row jacket, announced that he had had a lovely evening but was leaving since his driver was waiting out in the snow. As I have always said, the man was a true class act. We all miss him terribly.

OPPOSITE One of my wonderful memories of Bill Blass was his fondness for discovering beautiful things. This 19th-century French Majolica paté tureen is just such an object. Years later, I found it at the Christie's auction of his property. OVERLEAF LEFT AND RIGHT The dining area in the kitchen is the perfect example of my design philosophy in taking all surfaces into consideration. I love putting things where they are unexpected, like the roe deer horns around the skylight. The unusual French three-tier candle chandelier was found at the Marché aux Puces in Paris. The white English Ironstone pitcher in the center of the table was a house gift from Babe Paley to Slim Keith.

If you work hard enough, put in more time than others, and accomplish a good deal more than most in your field, then after a reasonable period of time you end up being labeled a legend or an icon. I have never really liked such titles, but must say that if ever such titles belong to anyone, I would think it would be Dawn Mello. It's strange that I don't remember the first time I met Dawn. It just seems she was always well-thought-of in our business and held in the highest regard. I would often see her at industry affairs. Always so attractive. Always dressed beautifully. I do remember the very first conversation I had with her. We were both invited to a cocktail party at the home of Kitty Hawks on Park Avenue. Kitty is the daughter of Slim Keith, who was one of my dearest friends. Kitty was also the daughter of the famous film director, Howard Hawks. Dawn was seated on the sofa alone, so I took the opportunity to introduce myself. Thank God the fashion designer Geoffrey Beene once confided to me years earlier how much he hated cocktail parties as much as I did, since he was also very shy, and said that he had figured out the perfect solution. When you just cannot say no and must go, get there very early and be sure to kiss and talk to the host first thing. Soon after the other guests start to appear, just disappear. I must say it works every time. But because of Dawn and Kitty, I stayed longer than was customary for me since I so enjoyed Dawn's company. That conversation started one of my most cherished friendships.

Soon after that cocktail party, I was appointed CEO of I. Magnin, based out of San Francisco. This was a crucial time for the store, which in its day had been the Bergdorf Goodman of the West Coast and one of the most prestigious high-end fashion specialty stores in the world, but which had also been losing money for many years. Its fortunes had begun to turn around by my predecessor, Rosemarie Bravo, a superb executive appointed by Ed Finkelstein when Macy's purchased I. Magnin in 1987.

My instincts told me that, as the new CEO, I could very well be the last chance I. Magnin had for survival. I was truly and completely petrified by my new position. This career move was never part of my master plan. I loved what I had been doing and had planned to die doing it.

So the very first thing I did before even moving to San Francisco, and after many helpful conversations with Rosemarie, was to call two top industry leaders for whom I had the greatest respect and admiration: Leonard Lauder, CEO of Estée Lauder, and Ira Neimark, former CEO of Bergdorf Goodman. Both had advanced their companies into high profitability, prestige, and double-digit volume increases, and both brilliantly understood the business of retailing particularly in terms of the high-end market.

I remember sitting at lunch with Ira one day, picking his brain. I was very honest about my reason for inviting him to lunch and told him that, since he and Dawn Mello ran the foremost specialty store in the world, I felt there was much I could learn from him. Ira went on and on as to what market and designer relationships he felt were necessary for a high-end specialty store, and why. Toward the end of our lunch, Ira looked at me very clearly and said, "Joe, after all was said and done I had something no one else had. I had Dawn Mello. You need a Dawn Mello, but I'm not sure there is another one out there. I kind of think not."

OPPOSITE Dawn Mello is a woman of impeccable taste and style. So when she decided she wanted to have a pet, she chose a beautiful black French poodle. Then named it Gina after Miss Lollobrigida. We called her Gina Lola Mello.

White Tea by the 17th Century

He went on to explain how he valued Dawn's natural instinct for what was right for Bergdorf Goodman, as well as what had to go. She was the merchandising and marketing conscience of the business, while he was the ultimate administrator and operations expert. Together, they made an amazing and accomplished team. There is no question in my mind that Bergdorf Goodman would not exist as the store it is today were it not for the talents and dedication of such outstanding executives.

It came as no surprise in our industry that, in 1989, the Gucci family finally realized that they needed serious fashion and merchandising expertise to help rejuvenate what was once the premier luxury brand in the world. And to deal with this serious situation, they first knocked on the door of Dawn Mello. Gucci had lost its way, taking its eye off the ball at the same time that the competition came in and dramatically eroded the brand's once dominant share of the luxury market.

Everyone considered it extremely smart back then for Gucci to go after the best. Not only was Dawn so very capable at high-end merchandising, but she also has an outstanding instinct for fashion trends, and the best eye around for product merchandising development and creative talent. She knew from the outset that she needed an exceptional talent to interpret her merchandising direction and to grow the Gucci business in a notoriously competitive arena. So Dawn went out and hired Tom Ford, offering him the position of creative director over all product and marketing. The name Tom Ford was a name that most had never heard of until Dawn and Gucci. Dawn and Tom's talents placed Gucci on top once again.

In 1994, Dawn left Gucci in the very capable hands of Tom's genius and was invited by Ira to rejoin Bergdorf. All of Dawn's New York friends were thrilled that she was coming back to New York. We could go back to our lovely little dinners and even catch a movie now and then. Finally, after another five years of hard work at Bergdorf Goodman, Dawn decided she wanted some time for herself and, much to the surprise of many, announced she would retire from the store.

So as Miss Mello, as she was always referred to, was planning her exit at Bergdorf's, people like Giorgio Armani, Oscar de la Renta, Ralph Lauren, and many others came knocking on her door from both sides of the Atlantic. As a result, Dawn Mello Associates was born in 1999.

Besides our many telephone calls each week, we know we will always be there for each other. On occasion, I am able to convince Dawn to come to Connecticut for a long weekend, which is like having one of your fondest relatives reappear—with wonderful goodies: amazing chocolate chip cookies or French macarons that are worth dying for. Or perhaps that wonderful smile that brings us such joy and sunshine. I do know one of my very favorite gifts is a divine, etched-glass Victorian celery goblet that I love using on the lunch table when I entertain. Guests will ask, "Where did you get that?" "Only the Dawn Mello eye could find that," is always my reply.

OPPOSITE Dawn Mello has always been a most welcome guest. Besides enjoying her company and wonderful conversations, she always arrived with the most creative gifts. This 19th-century etched glass celery goblet is one.

If anyone were to ask me how I would describe Jeffrey Banks, I would immediately respond: "A true gentlemen with impeccable taste." I would then add to my description that Jeffrey possesses an amazing memory. Truth is, he never seems to forget anything at all. Starting my career in the fashion and retailing business, I quickly became aware of Jeffrey's reputation for design excellence and impeccable standards of execution. Early on, the fashion industry recognized that he possessed a creative talent that transcended his youth. Appreciating that often less is more seemed to move his career in a direction that many young, aspiring talents to this day could only dream of.

Jeffrey's own dream started when he was only ten years old and confidently designing special-event clothing for his mother. And today, at 95, she is still a fashion plate. She instilled in her son, from an early age, an appreciation for quality and good design.

Unsurprisingly, Ralph Lauren quickly engaged Jeffrey as a design assistant for his studio on Day One of the start of Jeffrey's notable career. Unfortunately for Ralph, that would last only for a few years, since Calvin Klein also wanted Jeffrey. Jeffrey's career seemed to move forward with the best momentum imaginable—a momentum that would bring him to establish his own design studio and various licensing labels.

I would often see Jeffrey at the many industry functions we were both obliged to attend. Sadly, at the time, I never really knew him as a friend. I later found out that we coincidently shared a close friend. For over 30 years Jeffrey was the next-door neighbor and a dear friend in New York of Peggy Tagliarino, a friend of mine in Connecticut.

They seemed so compatible that they often came off as brother and sister rather than just good friends. They both shared many of the same interests, from a good book to the performing arts. But there is no doubt that their greatest joy was shopping relentlessly. They were two people who always saw the glass half full and would tirelessly look for ways of filling that preferred glass to the very top. All of Peggy's friends were well aware that she was never a morning person, while Jeffrey had always been an early riser. Knowing that Peggy loved to sleep in, Jeffrey would feel free to enter her apartment quietly every morning as she slept to take Peggy's dog Lilly out for a walk and pick up the morning papers.

Much to my joy, Peggy and Jeffrey were my guests for countless lunches and dinners. There are many things in my home that remind me of Jeffrey. One of them is the pleasure of using the divine antique napkins Jeffrey arrived with one afternoon, with no particular reason for bringing such a gift. The same might be said of the steak knives he arrived with another day because he simply adored their handles and knew I would, too.

Jeffrey has always been one of the most elegant and best-dressed men in New York. Absolutely impeccable. At a very young age, he was elected to the prestigious International Best-Dressed list. No surprise to me, since he always displayed such a natural style for putting himself together to true perfection.

OPPOSITE Slim Keith taught me long ago that a luncheon or dinner table need not always have flowers as a centerpiece but must still be entertaining. I found it much more fun creating new settings, such as the one with Jeffrey Banks' Irish napkins on Contagalli earthenware dishes, the artichoke-shaped peppermill from Missiaglia of Venice, and the bamboo-handled silverware by Buccelatti. Hopefully, I learned my lesson well and Slim would be pleased.

There are many things in my home that remind me of Jeffrey. One of them is the pleasure of using the divine antique napkins Jeffrey arrived with one afternoon, with no particular reason for bringing such a gift.

OPPOSITE In my mind, if Jeffrey Banks hadn't made it as an acclaimed fashion designer and author, there is no question that legendary Alex Trebek would have had serious competition from Jeffrey as the charming host of *Jeopardy*.

As CEO of I. Magnin, which was based in San Francisco, one of the perks I enjoyed was that I would often have the opportunity to meet some amazing people from all over. Fortunately for me, San Francisco had more than its fair share of wonderful natives in residence, and even luckier was that Robert and Margrit Mondavi were very much a part of this unique garden of Eden. For many, it has always been a must to experience the Napa Valley.

Although born in Minnesota, Robert moved to California with his family early on to attend high school in Lodi. He went on to graduate from Stanford University in 1937, with degrees in business administration and economics. Soon after, his father purchased the Charles Krug Winery in St. Helena, where it all started. Robert and his brother worked hard supporting their dad's dream and learning everything there was about the business. With Robert's added advantage of his business education, he saw greater opportunities and the potential to build a successful business of his own. He had a vision that Mondavi Vineyards could compete with the behemoths that dominated the French wine industry. With his family at his side, Robert accomplished his dreams, gaining the respect of so many people in Europe and the world over. He developed both a business and personal relationship with the legendary Baron Philippe de Rothschild, and they built up the prestigious Opus One Winery in Napa.

One of my main objectives as CEO of I. Magnin was to do almost anything to attract traffic into our Union Square store, where high-end fashion merchandising competition was fierce. Jessye Norman, the glorious opera star, was a friend, and one day she told me she was coming to San Francisco to perform for just one evening. She said she would be planning to spend the weekend in San Francisco, since she had a nephew in the area, and perhaps we could have dinner. I asked her if there was any chance I could interest her in doing a personal appearance on our designer floor at I. Magnin's. I would see to it that we had her most recent CDs at every register as a special tribute. Jessye agreed. Out of gratitude I suggested we plan a fun weekend, perhaps with a visit to Napa, where my divine friend Maria Mannetti Farrow, now Maria Mannetti Shrem, was a social force. Maria was not only very friendly with the Mondavis, she also had the most amazing house and small vineyard of her own, and was a very enthusiastic opera fan to boot. So when I shared with Maria that Jessye was coming to town, she took over the weekend plans and put Mondavi and Opus One on the agenda. Before the tour, we were guests of Bob and Margrit at their home for lunch.

Jessye loved the entire experience. While at Mondavi, Robert wanted to give us some wines and offered me three bottles of his coveted 1990 Cabernet Sauvignon Reserve. He knew that that was the year my son Christopher was born. Then he autographed each bottle for me and my son. Bob knew I did not drink very often, but when I did, this was always my wine of choice. I immediately thought that these bottles would never be opened until I had a reason to celebrate a major milestone in my son's life. Then when we went onto Opus One, and after the tour, Bob autographed another special bottle for Christopher and me. Yet nothing comes close to the memory of laughing and having lunch with dear friends sitting around a swimming pool, of all places in the center of their living room. Why not? They loved to swim.

OPPOSITE The parting gift from the Mondavis, after a memorable weekend in Napa, was these personalized bottles of 1990 Cabernet Sauvignon Reserve for Chris and me. They loved kids and shared the joy of Christopher in my life.

some wines and offered me three bottles of his coveted 1990 Cabernet Sauvignon Reserve. He knew that that was the year Christopher was born. Then he autographed the bottles for us.

OPPOSITE After a special tour of the Mondavi winery (which Robert Mondavi had created with the French banker and winemaker Guy de Rothschild), he gave me a personalized bottle of Opus One that I saved for Christopher ever since.

I never think of major celebrities or royal princes as having hobbies. Yet many well-known personalities throughout history have enjoyed a multitude of varied interests. For me, knowing that they do have hobbies makes them seem a good deal more real and a bit more approachable. When I was told that Princess Grace of Monaco was coming to Macy's, you could just imagine my surprise. This was in the fall of 1976. If royalty was to venture into a department store, chances were, back then, it would not have been Macy's. But fortunately for Macy's, Princess Grace had a hobby that allowed her time to enjoy her love of dried flower arranging and of creating floral collages that she would frame. During that visit, she shared with me that she actually found it very therapeutic when she was lonely for Prince Rainier, because they spent so much time apart. When learning of the Princess' passion, Springmaid, a clever bed and bath company, convinced the Princess to have her floral designs inspire a collection of bed linens, understanding before others the consumer appeal for celebrity-inspired merchandising. For the Princess, it was a win-win situation. She got to do what she loved and had the joy of seeing her creativity develop into an actual product. The main objective was to have all the profits go directly to her foundation.

The day of Her Royal Highness' personal appearance at Macy's was a much-anticipated event. The very first renovation in the Herald Square store was the sixth floor, which housed the entire domestic merchandising for Macy's, including the Bed and Bath Department. The visual merchandising staff had designed two room settings inspired by the designs Princess Grace had used for her collection of bed linens. I was asked to greet her when she arrived on the floor. I was very nervous. I had always thought she was about one of the most beautiful women I had ever seen. A crush of consumers and press awaited her arrival. We were introduced to each other and she was as lovely and gracious as one would expect. She turned to view her floral designs-inspired room and I could see that she was pleased. What made the rooms so exciting was the concept of using the linens on more than just the bed.

I never understood why more stores did not show the consumer how economical it was to use beautifully designed bed linens in creative ways. Headboards, walls, bedside chairs, as well as lampshades, skirted tables, and window treatments, could all be upholstered in the same fabric. After looking over the presentation, the Princess took my hand and kissed me. "Joe," she said. "I can't thank you and your staff enough. It is just beautiful, and much more than I expected. I must get photographs to show my husband. There are a few guest rooms I would like to use your ideas for when I return home." She asked me if I had ever visited Monaco. When I told her I had not, she insisted I do so, and soon. She promised to act as my tour guide. Wow! I thought. What an invitation. I never took her up on it. I was never much of a vacation person, and was not about to knock on the palace door.

A few weeks later, when I had returned to my office after some meetings, there was a package waiting for me next to my desk. It was a numbered lithograph signed by the Princess of one of her collage designs, with a lovely note. She signed it Princess Grace of Monaco and then over to the right, she signed it GPK. I later found out that Grace Patricia Kelly was her full name. What a lovely memory of a lovely experience with a lovely human being!

ABOVE Once I had the honor of being in the company of Grace Kelly and was able to develop a relationship with her. In my opinion, there was just no question that she was always meant to be royalty. She truly was a princess.

It was a numbered lithograph by the Princess of one of her collage designs, with a lovely note. She signed it Princess Grace of Monaco and then over to the right, she signed it GPK, her full name.

OPPOSITE Princess Grace of Monaco loved gardens and, as a result, undertook botanical collage art as a hobby. Her artistic accomplishments developed into a successful collection of bed linens with sales that benefited her charitable foundation. When she sent me this particular work of art as a gift, I was totally taken by surprise.

My first encounter with Thomas Messel started on the Macy's private jet, of all places. It was the early 1980s, and our company was on a roll. Ed Finkelstein had grown tired of the scheduling delays of the commercial airlines, which were costing us time and money, and so he did what many other multi-billion dollar businesses were doing: have Macy's buy its own Gulfstream. The hours spent by many of the executive team in the air in the privacy and comfort of the company airplane produced some of the most worthwhile discussions and decisions. The other great benefit was being able to offer important people the opportunity to travel in luxury, and network with them while enlisting their support, giving your brand a competitive edge.

One particularly memorable trip was on a flight to San Francisco. Ed had offered Bill Blass to fly with us purely in order to get him to do a personal appearance at I. Magnin there. Bill was already a good friend of mine and spending seven or so hours in his company was always guaranteed to be interesting and fun. On this occasion, the three of us were having a very good, businesslike conversation when, all of a sudden, Bill looked at Ed and said, "Why don't you guys do something with your antiques department? It's an embarrassment." Gulp, I remember thinking. Bill loved antiques and had a great eye, but I hadn't seen this one coming. Ed knew very little about antiques, and cared even less, although he definitely saw the department as an attraction. Ed knew that I shared Bill's interest and enthusiasm for art and antiques and so asked, "Joe, is that true?" "Ed, there's surely room for improvement," I said. It was the only response that I felt was honest and would hopefully not upset the staff back at the store. The problem with the merchandising of the antiques in what we called the Corner Shop was that it looked like just a lot of "stuff," with no particular point of view. The buyer had a very good eye but was not particularly creative and not aggressive to the benefit of his business. I always felt that he needed support and direction so that he could introduce a more interesting inventory. I felt the answer was to create environments on the selling floor by category, and that complete room settings would be much more inviting and entertaining than the existing piecemeal arrangement. "What you are proposing sounds like creative merchandising. Do it!" said Ed. "The Corner Shop now reports to you."

I had more than enough responsibility at that point and was reluctant to take on any more, but I also came from the old-fashioned school of business and believed that you should never refuse a request from your boss unless you were prepared to resign. I immediately began strategizing my plan of attack: Making the Corner Shop a destination in its own right, and also a profitable business. I decided that my first port of call would be Randy Ridless, one of my key creative designers with great taste, in New York. I phoned him as soon as we landed and immediately scheduled a trip to Europe to look for the distinctive merchandise that I felt would give us the best profit margins while creating an exciting buzz. On our first trip to the Macy's office in London, we were taken to meet Thomas Messel, a British furniture designer who was renowned for his high-quality reproductions, which I decided had to be part of our plan.

Visiting Thomas, his wife Pepe, and their four-year-old son, Hal, at Bradley Court in Wiltshire, their home and design studio, was one of the highlights of the trip. I adore England,

OPPOSITE A portrait of Slim Keith by Oliver Messel flanked by two watercolors of costume designs for a production of *Romeo and Juliet*, also by Messel, hang in the guest room. They were a gift from Thomas and Pepe Messel.

ABOVE Thomas Messel, author, furniture designer and historian, is also a direct descendent of Oliver Messel.
OVERLEAF LEFT AND RIGHT When I embarked on the new addition, every piece had to be planned for placement.
My collection of vintage intaglios from France, Italy, and England was meant to decorate the center stairwell.

so driving through the countryside to meet them was not exactly a hardship. It was winter, but English gardens look amazing throughout all four seasons and the gardens at Bradley Court, designed by Pepe, who was a very accomplished artist and landscape designer, were no exception. When Randy and I walked through Thomas' design studio, I began to realize what a truly creative genius he was. Not only did he have a unique understanding of period furniture, but he also had a special ability to combine creative talent with a passion for exceptional execution. We quickly realized that his collection contained many well-priced pieces of furniture that could do very well at Macy's. Thomas' understated and sincere manner gave us confidence in the viability of any purchase and, as our relationship grew, the process became one of pure joy. It also proved to be highly successful commercially. What became the exclusive Macy's Thomas Messel Collection would sell out quickly and reorders followed—the dream of any retailer or supplier.

Years later, when I was no longer at Macy's, I commissioned Thomas to make nine custom furniture pieces for Joan Rivers' new country house in Connecticut, which was down the road from Bill Blass and three minutes away from my home. I asked Thomas if he could find a subtle way of incorporating the monogram "JR" in the leaf-and-vine art design he'd created for her bedroom secretary and dresser. All nine pieces were amazing, and Joan was truly over the moon with them. Sadly, years later those pieces of furniture were auctioned at Christie's after Joan's tragic passing. I've often wondered if the new owner of the secretary or dresser was aware that Joan's initials are incorporated into the hand-done artwork on both pieces. Certainly he or she will never know the true joy that the furniture gave Joan, or the genius and craftsmanship of Thomas Messel that went into creating them.

Thomas is also the nephew of the celebrated English artist Oliver Messel, who excelled at everything from interior design to stage set design and costumes, and his own original works of art, from the 1940s through to his death in 1978. Thomas came to New York with Pepe for the American launch of his book on his uncle, Oliver Messel. Thomas' book is absolutely wonderful and presents in great detail many of his uncle's most creative accomplishments. By coincidence, I am also the proud owner of an original portrait that Oliver Messel did of Slim Keith in the 1960s, when Slim was married to Lord Kenneth Keith and living in England, many years before we became friends. It now hangs in my house in my favorite guest room, which I enjoy calling "The Lady Keith Suite." The jewel in that room's crown has always been the Messel portrait of Slim, which she gave me personally one day when we were sorting out her storage room at 32 East 64th Street in Manhattan. I love recalling the unceremonial presentation. She had the painting in a black plastic bag. Handing it to me, she said: "Here, you can have this if you like. It is a very good painting by Oliver Messel."

When Thomas and Pepe came to visit, they brought me two watercolor costume designs that Oliver had done many years earlier as a house gift. I immediately hung them in the guest room, one on either side of the Messel portrait of Slim. How amazing that my valued relationship with Slim introduced me to my cherished relationships with the Messel family that went on to involve the famous Joan Rivers. Three absolutely disparate entities came together through the joy of friendship.

In the early 1980s, we were really on a roll at Macy's. Many of us had begun to realize that we were part of something special and, after a good deal of hard work, Macy's had become the number-one choice for those seeking career opportunities in retail. Once again, the Macy's brand had become synonymous with excellence and professionalism. Many well-known leaders in corporate America started their careers in the training squad at Macy's. Often, during the normal course of my working day, I remember hearing about a department manager in our New Haven, Connecticut store by the name of Lou Amendola. It seemed that anyone who knew him spoke of him in the most glowing terms. I especially liked learning about talent in the branch stores, as I felt it helped ensure that the "Macy's story" was not always just about Herald Square.

I first met Lou in person on a visit to the New Haven store, where he was the department manager. All senior executives at Macy's—and especially those who valued their careers—knew that there was an unwritten mandate to travel to a different branch store every Friday. This was when CEO Edward S. Finkelstein would descend on a particular store to meet the store manager and discuss the nature of their business. At the same time, they could engage with some of the personnel, view the merchandising, and observe the customer profile. By each Thursday afternoon, Ed's office would have decided which store or two (and on some occasions, three) he would visit the following day. Once the word got out, it was always great fun to watch the various executives scrambling to change their plans so they could travel and run into the CEO in a given store—all "by coincidence," of course. The personnel in each store would often be up all night before a visit rearranging the selling floor with the hope of pleasing the visiting "suits" the next day. I always felt unannounced visits made more sense, which is what I usually did, whether it was Macy's or I. Magnin. Unfortunately, when you are close to six-foot five-inches tall, as I am, with very white hair, it's not so easy to critique a store unnoticed. God knows I have tried over the years.

New Haven seemed to attract more than its fair share of Macy's corporate executive visits. I quickly learned this was thanks to the presence of Pepe's Pizza. Pepe's was known as one of the best pizza restaurants on the East Coast. Ed Finkelstein loved to eat, and especially adored pizza, so Pepe's was an essential stop on any visit to New Haven. One Friday, I had driven to the New Haven store with Mike Stemen, who was then the director of all the branch stores as well as the flagship on Herald Square. There was a predictable pattern to these visits: The tone was often set by the buffet breakfast that opened proceedings and usually dictated how well or not the rest of the morning tour would play out. The entourage would involve eight or more executives, with the CEO and the usually-petrified store manager at the front, and everyone else trying to stay as close to the throne of power as possible. Despite what could be a nerve-wracking occasion for the store manager, everyone usually seemed to maintain a good sense of humor. This was largely due to Ed, who, although very smart and dedicated to the success of the business, always managed to keep business

OPPOSITE Lou Amendola's surprise Christmas gift of a pair of antique black-and-white ivory hourglasses sit on the hall game table. In the frame leaning on the wall is a rare photograph of my two dear friends, Slim Keith and Babe Paley, who are playing chess. Slim once confided that Babe was the only woman she was ever intimidated by.

issues in perspective and not take things too seriously. "Grace under pressure" was one of his favorite sayings. But I also experienced many a day when grace was on holiday.

One morning, when we entered an area in the store called The Action Shop, a casual merchandising category for young men, the department manager was called forward to meet the suits and brief us on the state of his business. He was obviously nervous—not surprising, considering his audience. I remember thinking: Here is the legendary Louis Amendola. Yes, there is no question he is Italian. He looked like ten cousins I had, back in Brooklyn. I never knew they had Italians in New Haven, but have since learned that there is a big Italian community there. I guess that explains Pepe's Pizza. Our visit to his department went very well, as he seemed to know his business and was able to answer any questions. Everyone walked away feeling that The Action Shop business was in very capable hands. So much so that a few months later, Lou was no longer working in the New Haven store but had been promoted to assistant buyer in the men's division at Herald Square.

I didn't get to know Lou well until many years later, when we coincidentally both ended up at the Donna Karan Company. By that point, Lou's career had moved up nicely and he was now Vice-President of Men's Merchandising, working for another former Macy's colleague, Linda Beauchamp, who was President of DK Men's. Donna had recruited me to be President of her Donna Karan retail and store planning divisions. Today, Lou's talents have taken him to an impressive position as Chief Merchandising Officer for Brooks Brothers worldwide. But I have no doubt that his promotion to the buying office at Macy's was his winning lottery ticket. Lou would be the first to acknowledge the greatest benefit of his move to 34th Street was that it gave him the opportunity to work and travel with Bruce Binder, the Men's Fashion Director.

Lou and I come from very similar Italian backgrounds and I understand perfectly that, while always "Lou" to those who know and love him, he will always be Louis to his mother and father, and that is just how it will remain. He is a most loving son, brother, nephew, and friend, and has no idea how really Italian he is at times. Take Lou into a good Italian restaurant and put a plate of pasta in front of him and he immediately becomes Louis, the Italian kid from the Italian neighborhood of New Haven. Over the years, Lou and I became very close. I remember the day he called and said he was taking a ride up to my part of Connecticut and wanted to buy a house. I was very surprised and figured he wanted a day in the country and a reason to be there by looking at houses. I lined up a few I thought were worthwhile but knew there was no chance he would buy anything. But at about four o'clock that afternoon, he had purchased a home about two miles from me. I was in shock, and overjoyed. I helped Lou and his father transform his new purchase into one of the best houses in the best location in our county.

In the fall of 2005, I was living in London as CEO of Penhaligon's and Lou surprised me with a visit while he was on a business trip for Brooks Brothers. We both share a great interest in antiques, and happened to discover that Sotheby's was holding a sale of Elton John's things from his London home. We went to the preview together and, as we looked around, we each made notes of things that caught our eye. We left silent bids and moved on. The following Christmas, Lou surprised me with a pair of ivory hourglasses that had come out of that Elton John auction. I had admired them at the preview, but was trying to be good and passed on them. They now sit in my living room and often remind me of Lou's generosity.

ABOVE My friend Lou Amendola's strong instinct for stylish clothing has guided him through an impressive career in retailing that has now brought him to the position of Chief Merchandising Officer for Brooks Brothers.

There is no question that Kenneth J. Lane is one of my all-time favorites on the list of close friends and personalities. Kenny, to his close friends, was truly a contradiction. When meeting him for the first time, one would usually walk away with the impression that he was very grand and a bit standoffish. But not only was he one of the most gifted jewelry designers in modern times, he was also one of the sweetest, kindest, most generous, humorous, and intelligent gentlemen. I loved being in his company, even if it was just us boys visiting at Mortimer's with Glenn Bernbaum for brunch on a Sunday. Glenn and Bill Blass were buddies and as hard as it is to believe, their friendship started while serving in the United States Army together.

In the early days, Bill and Glenn were always lending Kenny money and then would complain that he would often forget to pay them back. Saving for a rainy day was not a concern for Kenny. God would provide, or if not God, then Glenn or Bill. From Day One, he enjoyed the finer things in life. The minute he accumulated a bit of cash, he was off to some exotic place to be a houseguest of royalty or a celebrity. He could also be found at Christie's bidding on a fine Renaissance painting to add to his vast art collection. To be entertained in his apartment on Park Avenue was a treat. One afternoon, he invited me with my 12-year-old son for lunch. When I was not looking, he would slip Christopher small amounts of red wine, acting like an irresponsible uncle. At that particular luncheon, Christopher happened to mention that someday he wanted to have a velvet suit. Kenny left the table and returned minutes later with a salmon-colored velvet suit that had been his as a young man, presenting it to Christopher as a gift. It fit Christopher perfectly and still hangs here in our closet.

Kenny had strong relationships with untold numbers of friends across the planet. The list could start at Buckingham Palace and go on to the deli on the corner of East 35th Street and Madison Avenue. He loved people and everyone loved him. My country house was within walking distance of the socialite Barbara Mortimer's, a close friend of Kenny's. Kenny and the divine Mary McFadden would often come to Barbara's for the weekend. Once, I was invited to a Saturday night dinner party since Kenny, Mary, and John Richardson would also be there.

If you were invited for 8 pm, Barbara usually would not come down before 9. She could very possibly be on the property feeding the local raccoon population, which she did diligently each evening. Barbara was a total eccentric and divine—directly out of a 1930s Hollywood movie. That evening, I decided to take my time getting there and arrived about 9:15 pm, since I knew dinner would not be served until 10 or 10:30. As I entered, a concerned Barbara asked me if I would see why Kenny was having difficulty in the kitchen with the leg of lamb. I found him standing in front of the oven brandishing a meat fork, a full glass of scotch in one hand, and a cigarette in the other. It was obvious that the scotch was not Kenny's first of the night. He said, "I can't figure out why I can't get this leg of lamb to cook." I told him it was always helpful if you turned the gas on first. We made scrambled eggs and hash browns and had the best laugh. To sit at a dinner table with such personalities was an experience I could never take for granted. I was always afraid that I would wake up from this wonderful dream.

PREVIOUS PAGES The 19th-century Carrera marble bust of a young Augustus Caesar has traveled a good deal, including from an auction house in London to my house in Connecticut. OPPOSITE The custom-made Savile Row salmon-colored dinner suit was a gift to Christopher from Kenneth J. Lane one day while we three were enjoying a lovely lunch at Kenny's Manhattan apartment. I always found it such fun to think that Kenny once fit into the suit.

Kenny left the table and returned minutes later with a salmon-colored velvet suit on a hanger that had been his as a young man, presenting it to my son as a gift. Christopher was delighted.

OPPOSITE Kenneth J. Lane, left, who was as comfortable in the company of royalty as he was with just Chris and me, joined Vanessa Williams and First Lady Nancy Reagan at a New York black-tie event in the early 1980s. Those of us who were close to him would often call him by his nickname of "Mr. Social." There was just no one he didn't know.

Philip Lawshe was a bit of a peacock and had every right to be. He was one of the most beautiful men I had ever seen—impeccably groomed, with great big blue eyes and an irresistable smile. When not working, he lived at his gym and had a body even Hercules would have envied. He was also a sweetie with a great sense of humor. I inherited Philip when I was promoted to Director for Branch Stores at Lord & Taylor, and Philip was the Visual Merchandising Manager at the Lord & Taylor store in Atlanta. Philip was also a southerner and had the charm of most southern gentlemen. Philip would often have small dinner parties at his beautiful apartment on Peachtree Avenue in Atlanta. I love going to the homes of friends for the first time. It can be a very revealing experience and Philip did not disappoint me with his great sense of style.

The first time I went to visit Philip at his spacious apartment, he greeted me with a big bear hug and insisted immediately on giving me the grand tour. I will never forget his bedroom—sparsely furnished with everything—walls, ceiling, moldings, and doors—painted the most beautiful shade of deep grey. Philip's bed seemed to be floating in the middle of the room. There was no headboard and I admired the perfectly focused lighting. The bed was raised above the floor and I noticed that there were a number of what looked like photograph albums neatly stacked under the box spring. I asked Philip what that was about. I assumed he had cherished pictures of family and friends and I was sort of correct. I think I was supposed to notice. We sat on the edge of the bed and one by one he proudly took out the albums and shared the photographs with me. Nearly every picture was of Philip taken by serious professionals or at gatherings with friends. He seemed to have had a wardrobe that went from jeans and muscle shirts to black-tie attire. There was not one photograph without Philip in it. I remember thinking this was one of the funniest things I had ever seen. I didn't think it was about ego with Philip at all. He just truly liked himself.

We went on to work together for a good number of years and had a great deal of fun and even a bit of drama. Then our careers moved on in different directions and about 15 years later, I got a call from Philip at Macy's asking to see me. He arrived looking as handsome as ever and as impeccably dressed as I remembered. The years had been good to him I thought. He said he had just moved to New York and needed a job and wondered if there could possibly be an opportunity for him at Macy's. We talked for a while remembering wonderful times and then went on to discuss what he thought he could contribute to our organization and what he was hoping to accomplish, both short- and long-term, with his career.

In less than a week's time, I arranged for Philip to interview with a few of my executives at Macy's to see if there was an opportunity for him in our organization. It would be their decision, not mine. In short order, a position was identified and after so many years I wanted the fun of giving him the good news and seeing his reaction. At that meeting, as it became obvious to him that I was offering him a position at Macy's, he started to tear up. I assumed he was moved by the opportunity until he got up, closed my office door, and sat back facing me in front of my desk trying very hard to compose himself. "Joseph," he said, "let me present a hypothetical situation to you. Would you still offer me the position if you knew I was HIV

OPPOSITE This 19th-century tortoise shell framed mirror was left to me by Philip Lawshe, showing how thoughtful he could be, and how well he remembered that he had admired my collection of small antique tortoise shell objects.

ABOVE There was no question that one of my associates at Macy's, Philip Lawshe, loved the camera. There was also no question that the camera loved him back. And with good reason. His natural smile was genuine and infectious. OVERLEAF A close friend walked in my bedroom during a house tour, took one look around and said, "Oh, I guess we are in the Throne Room." I loved it. The canopied-bed room is really my own personal cocoon, where I can truly spend days without leaving. PAGES 222–223 The 17th-century wax statue of Saint Joseph on the bedroom chest was a gift from Silvano and Loise Picchi. My collection of small icons dates from the 13th to the 19th centuries.

positive?" I was stunned. I tried to think this horror through quickly without showing what I felt inside. Instantly, that horrendous feeling of one's blood running cold came over me. I tried desperately not to let my face show how I felt. Unfortunately, it was not a new experience for me, having been only too often in similar situations. With all he had to deal with, he could still be honest. He still looked perfectly healthy and I would never have known then if not for his display of a true and honest conscience. What he was desperate for at that point was health insurance for the inevitable time he feared, like so many others, would be his destiny. I said that, as much as I wanted, I could not make this decision on my own, but I could promise him that I would do everything in my power to see if I could make it happen. It was a different time and early on for corporate America in dealing with this horror. After he left my office with a heartfelt hug, I immediately went to the head of our human resources division, closed his office door, and explained the entire situation, urging him as much as I could to please give me the go-ahead to make this happen for this young man. I knew our human resources director very well. I could tell he wanted to say, "Do it," but felt he had to go to our CEO. I only insisted I go along with him, knowing it would be more difficult for him to say no with me there. So we pleaded our case to Edward S. Finkelstein, and I could feel his eyes on me as he struggled to make a decision. After a bit of discussion among the three of us, he turned to me and said "OK, do it." There have been few times I remember being that happy and depressed at the same time. I called Philip and asked him if he could have dinner. I wanted him to know he was not dealing with this alone any longer and had yet another friend who cared deeply and would be at his side. "So when can you start?" I said, after we reviewed the menu. He was over the moon with joy. Wow, I remember thinking, I have no right to complain about anything in my life. As soon as Philip came to Macy's he almost immediately became part of the family. I would see him from time to time and was so pleased that he was happy, looking healthy, and by all reports liked by everyone he encountered. I also unfortunately remember the horror of those years having nine or ten other young men I knew that I would pray for every evening name by name. Something deep inside my being urged me to say their names aloud: Glenn, Billy, James, Philip, Jim, Bruce, Vincent, Art, and Price. Over time, the list seemed to get shorter and shorter until it was no more.

About a year or two after Philip started at Macy's, he became ill. Little by little he got progressively worse until he could not work any longer. Philip was blessed with a lovely and wealthy gentleman friend in Dallas, Texas, who had him come to live with him, to be sure Philip got the 24/7 care he needed. I talked to Philip and his amazing friend every single day including the morning of the day he passed away. Philip was inspirational in dealing with his illness. He seemed to be able to handle it all with total grace. Gone was the peacock but the same lovely man I knew was still there to ease the pain. Months after Philip's death, his Dallas friend called to say that Philip had left Christopher and me a few things in his will. Philip knew I loved antique tortoise shell, so he gave me his beautiful 18th-century tortoise shell framed mirror. I adore it, not because it is tortoise shell, but because I know Philip, the peacock, used it often. Now I look at it every morning as I walk out of my bedroom to start my day. It's such a good feeling to know that I am looking into the same mirror he often did.

ABOVE A few years ago, I enjoyed spending time with Loise and Silvano Picchi, one afternoon in Palermo, Italy, while discovering my family roots. Their smiles are natural and not meant just for the camera, one of the reasons I love them.

One day, much to my good fortune, I learned that R.H. Macy's, Inc., had a buying office in Florence, Italy, perhaps my second favorite city in Europe. It was one of the cities I had traveled to as a young man during my first trip to Europe at the insistence of my mentor, Cici Kempner. On my first visit, I fell in love with everything about Florence—at least everything I could experience on my limited budget at the time. It was magical from the start. When alone, I did my favorite thing—walking, walking, and walking some more. I visited every museum, gallery, and shop I could get into for free. Once I found myself standing in complete awe in front of Botticelli's *The Birth of Venus*—done in the late 1400s. When hungry, I would buy some Italian bread in a local bakery, a piece of cheese, and perhaps some prosciutto, and would find a spot with a spectacular view to enjoy my heavenly meal. On a few evenings, Cici had friends there and they would invite me to have dinner with them at their home or in a local trattoria.

Years later, Macy's managed to make Florence even more special. The buying office was very important for the corporation and strategically located in the middle of the city. Macy's had a very strong, and as a result, large volume of business in the hard-goods categories in each of their American department stores. Housewares, tabletop, and leather accessories were the most important. The Florence office manager was a gentleman who defied description. Forty years ago, he might have been good looking, but at the time he was considerably overweight. He had the reputation of being very intelligent, and had the managerial and personal talents of a bull in an outdoor food market. To my amazement, he was completely oblivious to the real world of business and the people around him. Later, I came to the conclusion that he was smart enough to know that he needed to surround his own inadequacies with great talent and ability—which he did with his department managers, the most important of whom was Silvano Picchi. I have been told that Florence is somewhat like San Francisco. Just about anyone you meet there is not from there. Silvano and his wife Loise were two of the very few true natives of that city. It did not take long before we all became friends. Loise retired from Macy's many years before Silvano did the same. She dedicated her time to her young family and opened antiques shops in the city.

Whenever I traveled to Florence, it was always to work with our merchants in the tabletop factories, designing and sourcing the best and most competitively priced products for our gift and housewares divisions. We were constantly looking for inspiration. I have a great eye for detail so that on a walk on any street in the city I would find a treasure of inspiration. One afternoon, Silvano took me to the showroom of a famous ceramic manufacturer that dated back to the Medicis. Piles of treasures were all over the place. There were even pieces of authentic Della Robbia. I begged Silvano to find out if I could buy a few of the antiques. But after a long discussion in passionate Italian, Silvano reported that it was not possible. The antiques were not for sale. I left disappointed but not defeated. Over time, Silvano worked his magical charm and as a result I have been able to enjoy three pieces for over 30 years. On another visit to Florence, as we walked down a street with many little shops, I spotted an icon in a window. Instead of the typical saintly figure of most religious icons, there was an animal head on a human form. Silvano knew the complete history of the 13th-century icon of Saint Guinefort that now holds a place of honor in my collection. But Loise and Silvano will always hold a place of honor in my heart because of the memories we shared.

On another visit to Florence, I spotted an icon in a window. Instead of the typical saintly figure of most religious icons, there was an animal head on a human form.

OPPOSITE After hours of walking the streets of Florence, Silvano and I passed an antiques shop with this ram's head icon in the window. The 13th-century icon of St. Guinefort was something I had never seen before. Of course, Silvano knew the complete history. He was also a very effective negotiator—the reason the icon is now mine. OVERLEAF LEFT The pair of chairs in the master bedroom are covered in emerald green silk mohair because, many years ago, the interior designer Angelo Donghia told me that was a must. Knowing how expensive the fabric was, I said, "OK, just send me the fabric." A bolt of 30 yards arrived the next day. OVERLEAF RIGHT Thinking out of the box is truly one of the talents I respect most. When my upholsterer said he could not cover the chaise with the oriental carpet I wanted to use, I told him I knew he could. He did. I love knowing it is a one-of-a-kind piece. PAGES 230–231 The red Rubelli sofa was the centerpiece of Bruce Binder's apartment. He was proud of it because his friend, French interior designer Jacques Grange, had created it. The lamps are vintage Fortuny. The military profile portrait came from the estate of Bill Blass. Slim Keith would say the spot was perfect for reading a good book.

February 2, 1976, was my first day at Macy's in New York—at the time maybe the most petrifying day of my relatively short career. I found the world's largest store to be absolutely frightening and overwhelming. So much so that, within a day or so of arriving, I believed I had made the biggest mistake of my young working life. Macy's was a sharp contrast from the lovely, small, dignified, quiet, and familiar Lord & Taylor where my career had started.

The Herald Square store had not seen any renovations since the Great Flood of 1913. Every floor had bargain table merchandise with everything from cheap flatware—five pieces for a dollar—to socks and ladies' bras in about every aisle on every floor. Only a union member was allowed to move a fixture on the selling floor. If an executive tried, they were immediately reported and the complaint was filed with the union representative. Every evening, security people with guard dogs walked the floors and stockrooms to be sure no homeless people spent the night in the store. It was a grim picture and a sharp contrast from the Lord & Taylor on Fifth Avenue. Yet Macy's was known as the number one tourist attraction in New York. I had to keep reminding myself of this and to be aware that, since it was so bad and had fallen so far down, and that I had been presented with the challenge of a lifetime.

Unsurprisingly, it was impossible to attract good executive talent in just about any area of the organization in the early years. But none of this seemed to slow down Ed Finkelstein's resolve to position Macy's once again as the prime retailer in New York and on the East Coast. And then the nation and perhaps even the world. It was just a matter of time. It was easy to see that he was quickly building a formidable team that could bring forth his dream. But for creative people, visual people, my people, it was a different story. Many of them would often laugh when I would try to convince them that Macy's was about to change and become the most exciting store in the world. At the time, anyone of any worth in the retail industry wanted to be at Bloomingdale's. High-end vendors in the retail marketplace would not even return calls from Macy's executives.

Amazingly, there was already a handful of outstanding merchandising talents at Macy's when Finkelstein arrived as CEO in the New York executive offices, but they needed his capable direction, strategic encouragement, and professional support to get the job done. One of those talents was an executive in the merchandising area of the housewares division by the name of Terry Mottoros. She came straight out of college and went directly to work in the world's largest store. She was very intelligent and totally loyal to Macy's. Terry loved working with Art Reiner, then Senior Vice-President for half of the stores. And Art grew quickly to respect all that Terry brought to the success of his division.

On my first day, I was asked to come to the fifth floor to meet the administrator for housewares. That division wanted to make a merchandising move on the selling floor and needed people from my team to accomplish their goals. The administrator was Terry Mottoros and she was very difficult. I could not believe my eyes when I walked the floor. It required no great talent on my part to quickly see that the standards of stock keeping, fixtures, and

OPPOSITE If I had to pick my own zodiac sign it would be Leo. Thanks to good timing, it was just meant to be. Terry Mottoros went to great pains in England to surprise me for my birthday with this engraving of a mother lion with her cubs. The French, crown-shaped light fixture is from the estate of Joan Rivers. I had purchased it for her house years before her passing. She loved it, so when it came up for auction years later I knew I had to have it.

merchandise presentation on the selling floor were less than impressive. It took me no time to make Terry aware of how poorly I felt it looked. We proceeded to have a rather unpleasant exchange of words in the middle of the selling floor itself, and I must say, I was very grateful that our first encounter did not take place in the cutlery area. I went back to my office very upset, and asked my team who in the world was that crazy woman on the housewares floor? They knew instantly that it could only be Ms. Mottoros.

I love remembering that, somehow, Terry and I progressed beyond that initial exchange into an exceedingly productive working relationship. Terry and I went on to travel to many parts of the world together, identifying resources that could meet the merchandising needs of the future Macy's Cellar, a housewares–merchandising concept as a street of shops, a concept that Ed had brought with him from California. Finkelstein led with his greatest strength. Home! The entire housewares division fell under Terry's supervision.

So Art, Terry, and myself, supported by our staffs and some very capable outside consultants, went to work creating the Macy's New York Cellar. I thought it needed to be a good deal more sophisticated for the New York East Coast and be competitive at the same time. But Ed was not good with change and felt California was perfect. The three of us finally got him to agree to a major upgrade of the Cellar concept and environment. The Cellar opened to the public on a Monday morning in October, 1976. There was truly nothing like it in New York, or in the country. As the opening store bell went off and customers started flooding the floor, I turned and noticed that Terry was actually crying for joy. I got to a phone and interrupted the executive committee meeting, asking to have Ed take my call. I nervously proceeded to remind him that this was the morning of the Cellar opening and how emotional it was for Terry and many others. I also suggested that perhaps he might consider coming down to the Cellar for a few minutes since I knew it would mean so much to Terry and her team after months and months of almost 24/7 dedication to making his vision of the Cellar a reality. His response was very gracious and appreciative. Minutes later, he led his group of executives down ten floors to the Cellar esplanade where Terry was standing. When she turned and saw Ed and Art, I thought she was about to die. After Ed went back to his meeting, Terry kept repeating, "I just can't believe he remembered and came down." I just smiled.

Then the discussion that we knew would come sooner or later finally arrived. It was decided that it was time to attack the main floor of the Herald Square store. A retail brand can have only one flagship and the world's first impression to that flagship would often dictate how the different industries would perceive that brand. Finally, one sleepless night, it came to me. This could not be approached as a renovation. It had to be approached as a restoration of a flagship icon. Macy's Herald Square, with its over 100 years of history, could not be just another retail store redo with updated fixturing and lighting. No one was ever allowed to use the term "renovation" in my company. There were so many talents that contributed tirelessly to this goal, and while it's difficult to single out just one, I must. Carl Polino was head of store planning and a total planning genius. No project was greater in both our minds than the main floor, and Carl

OPPOSITE Terry Mottoros and Jack Straus, right, the grandson of Isadore Straus of the Macy-Straus family, joined me on a cold day in 1976, the year I had started at Macy's, to watch the already legendary Macy's Thanksgiving Day Parade.

got it in an instant. Carl made my responsibility a good deal easier due to his amazing talent and lack of ego. All I ever had to do was dream and walk away. I knew Carl would always find a way to make my dream a reality and he always did. He never disappointed me. Never!

Due to Terry's success with the Cellar and other areas of merchandising, she was now Senior Vice President for much of the merchandising on the main floor. It took more than two years of planning and construction to complete the restoration of the Heard Square main floor. We could look back and feel we did a pretty outstanding job, but never did until we knew that the numbers and the return on investment were paying off.

After many complimentary articles about the excitement at Macy's, and the many talented people there, the only piece of press we ever received that put me over the moon was an article written by Paul Goldberger, the architectural critic of the *New York Times*. In an article published on December 1, 1983, he got it perfectly. He understood, and saw that although the business needed a renovation to enhance the merchandising and increase sales by updating the floor, it was right to approach the project as a restoration.

Two elaborate evenings were planned to introduce the new main floor to the retail market and press. For these two black-tie galas, I wanted something unusual and special that hopefully would remain with guests for many years to come. Through Ruth Schwartz, the public relations director, we commissioned a French artist who is known by the name of Razzia, to do a painting associated with the main floor restoration so that we could give each and every guest a signed and numbered lithograph. I had the original work of art hung in Art's office, as the restoration had taken place under his watch.

At one point, Terry was appointed CEO of the Macy's Atlanta division. Art Reiner called me to discuss gift ideas that the New York division might consider for Terry's new appointment. I immediately pointed to the Razzia painting. Terry was overjoyed and had the painting sent to her new office in Atlanta. Terry and I always remained very close. Even after her retirement from Macy's we would talk almost every day. One day, the unthinkable happened. I was unable to reach Terry by phone for three or four days and it was extremely unusual for her not to return my calls within hours. Finally, her husband Pete called from St. Vincent's hospital to tell me Terry had been admitted and had been diagnosed with cancer. She went on to suffer for over five years. On her very last visit to my home in Connecticut, Pete drove up in a large SUV and, with Terry comfortably inside, I saw him carrying a large framed something into my house. It was the original painting by Razzia. Pete confided that Terry knew this would be her last Christmas with us and very much wanted to know that the painting would be with me. No work of art could ever hold so many memories of such special times spent while sharing such cherished relationships.

OPPOSITE French artist Razzia painted an original work that now hangs in my home gym, of Macy's iconic main floor, to commemorate the brand's 125th anniversary. The painting also reminds me of the tragic loss of a beloved friend and colleague, Terry Mottoros, who gave it to me as a Christmas gift the year she knew would be her last.

* Myra and Edward S. Finkelstein: Ed's vision made Macy's great and gave me a stage on Broadway to do my thing. Myra's love made me feel like a family member.

* Arthur and Tara Diedrick: Their inspiring love for each other and shared wisdom for all brings to those of us fortunate to be considered friends, gifts of untold value.

* Suzanne Slesin, Frederico Farina, and Kelly Koester, at Pointed Leaf Press: They saw something in me and my journey I would never have been able to see to this day. Without their wisdom, instinct, creativity, and professional expertise there would surely be no *Friends* *Bearing Gifts*. Thank you also to Antoine Bootz and Anne Day for their beautiful photographs.

* Joan and Jerry Adler: Wherever they might be on the planet at any given time, there is tremendous comfort knowing they are but an e-mail or phone call away. Unless of course they are in Mexico.

* Cynthia Lewis: One of the great talents in the publishing arena and, to my good fortune, a long-time friend who brought me to Suzy Slesin's doorstep. I will always be grateful.

* My monastic brothers: Weston priory was my home for a few years and the monks there have been my extended family since 1962. Knowing they are there for me with love and prayers has never failed to get me through the most difficult times. To this day, being there was the closest thing to experiencing heaven on earth.

* James O'Shea and Charles Kufferman: Through their amazing talents and love at the West Street Grill in Litchfield, Connecticut, I am guaranteed to be always well-fed, as I always have been.

* Rose Quint: A quiet and most-valued support as a friend and the sanity essential for me to function on a daily basis at my computer.

* To my wire hair terriers, Asta and Piper: Their faces, patience, and unfaltering love makes the lows a lot easier for me to climb out of.

* And to so many, many more, who, perhaps not singled out in these pages, played, and continue to play, no small part in making my journey the adventure it has become. Their unselfish love and support are exactly what made this book happen and each day worth living.

–Joseph Cicio, March, 2018

INDEX

JOSEPH CICIO was born in Brooklyn, New York, into an Italian-American family. He then followed monastic studies at St. Paul's Abbey in Newton, New Jersey, and Western Priory, in Weston, Vermont and graduated from the New York School of Interior Design in New York. Cicio has been the Director of Visual Merchandising for the Lord & Taylor branch stores; the Corporate Senior Vice President for Creative Services and Product Development at R.H. Macy's in New York; the Chairman and CEO of I. Magnin in San Francisco, California; the President of Retail Development for Donna Karan, Inc.; the President of Retail Development for Sun International; the CEO of Mayors Jewelry; the CEO for Penhaligon's worldwide; the European Director for Erno Laszlo; and a marketing consultant for numerous fashion and home furnishings brands worldwide. Cicio currently lives in Litchfield County, Connecticut. *Friends* *Bearing Gifts* is his first book. For more information, or to contact Joseph Cicio, please visit JosephCicio.com.

PHOTOGRAPHY CREDITS Unless noted below, the photographs are from the private collection of Joseph Cicio or courtesy of the subjects. Every effort has been made to locate the holders of copyright; any omissions will be corrected in future printings. COVER ART Ernesto Artillo; COVER PHOTOGRAPHS Lauren Bacall: Ron Galella/Getty Images; Audrey Hepburn: Time Life Images/Getty Images; Joan Rivers: Josiah Kamau/Getty Images; INTERIORS PHOTOGRAPHS Antoine Bootz; PAGE 4 Francesco Scavullo; PAGE 14 Courtesy of Lord & Taylor; PAGES 32–39, 48, 49, 54–55 Anne Day; PAGE 197 Ron Galella/Getty Images; PAGE 208 Matt Conte, courtesy of Brooks Brothers.

FRONT AND BACK MATTER CAPTIONS PAGES 2–3 The writer Truman Capote, who hosted the Black and White Ball at the Plaza Hotel in New York on November 28, 1966, an event now known as one of the most memorable parties of all time, insisted on having his best lady friend, Nancy "Slim" Keith at his side at the star-studded evening. OPPOSITE TITLE PAGE In 1994, I was seated next to Sophia Loren, the Italian movie star, at the Japanese fashion designer Issey Miyake's show in Paris. OPPOSITE DEDICATION American fashion photographer Francesco Scavullo took this portrait of me with my son, Christopher, in around 1994. OPPOSITE CONTENTS On my birthday in 1980, my friend David Leong made my dream of owning a Modigliani a reality with this engraving of a nude that now hangs in my Connecticut home. ABOVE The photograph of my beloved wire hair terriers, Piper, Topper, Spencer, and Asta was taken in 1985. When guests would visit, they would hold court and not move. At first glance, many people would assume they were not real. It did not take them long to realize they were actually very real. PAGE 241 The amazing singer Jessye Norman accompanied me to the opera in San Francisco, in 1993. No royalty could ever command as dramatic and regal a presence. To be at her side was nothing less then a dream.

Publisher: Suzanne Slesin
Creative Director: Frederico Farina
Managing Editor: Kelly Koester
ISBN: 978-1-938461-96-5
Library of Congress number: 2018933563
Printed in Italy / First Edition

My friends: Randy Bill Stacy Bruce Bobby Maria [
Jesse Tye Betty Henry James Gigi Caroline Jerry P
Richard Marie Patrick Norman Francis Stephen N
Wendy Estelle Mark Linda Bob Allen Vera Frank Leo
Beth Kathleen Gilda Pete Rosemarie Debbie Geri
Robin Mike Jeffrey Maureen John Arthur Linda Ce
Russell Susan Martin Edith Margie Eleanor Nan Tor
Nancy Phyllis Dick Allen Ludwig George Robert J
Elliot Mica Estee Glenn Don Joe Marilyn Matthew
Marvin Mark Massimo Jim Ed Pamela Ruth Myra
Ann Vicky Catherine Naomi Arland Herb Mindy J
Lee Teresa Chet Drew Stan Seymour Margot Nick
Alistair Ashley Scott Carolyn Elsa David Stephan
Charles James Roberts Adrienne Ward Nico Ken
Pat Robin Seth May Lenni Jacqui Boaz Brent M
Bernadine Jesse Ira Donald Emile Howard Joel Pr
Judy Claudia Elizabeth Carl Victor Ralph Rene Yve
Ellen Reed Russell Sofia Will Rose Debbie Milos Pep
Edward Jeffrey Cliff Robin Blanche Anne Vanessa